THE ROLE OF MULTINATIONAL COMPANIES IN LATIN AMERICA

ECSIM publications

already published:

The Rôle of Multinationals in a New International Order (a debate), 1977, English and French, 44 p.

Codes of Conduct for Multinational Companies: Issues and Positions, H. Schwamm and D. Germidis, 1977, English and French, 72 p.

Values and Limitations of Codes of Conduct as Regulating Instruments for Multinational Corporations, a symposium held at Louvain-La-Neuve, Belgium on 5 and 6 October 1977.

Multinational Corporations: the E.C.S.I.M. Guide to Information Sources, J.O. Mekeirle, 1977 multilingual, 454 p.

How and Why Companies Become Multinational, M. Delapierre, Ch. A. Michalet, 1978, English and French, 33 p.

Who's Afraid of the Multinationals? A Survey of European opinion on Multinational Corporations, J. Attali, M. Holthus, D. Kebscull, G. Péninou, 1978, English and French, 207 p.

To be published in 1979.

The International Division of Labour and Multinational Companies, M. Tharakan and a symposium.

Multinational and Development in Black Africa: A Case Study in the Ivory Coast, J. Masini, M. Ikonicoff, C. Jedlicki and M. Lanzarotti.

Europe + Latin America + the Multinationals: A positive sum game for the exchange of raw materials and technology in the 1980s, B. Lietaer.

Investment and Divestment Policies of Multinational Corporations in Europe, D. Van Den Bulcke, J.J. Boddewyn, B. Martens and P. Klemmer.

European Integration and the Multinational Corporations, H. Schwamm.

Dynamic Aspects of US Multinational Operations in Europe, S. Young and N. Hood.

Rural Development and the Multinational Corporations — Columbia and the Cameroons, C. Goux, S. Fayman and C. de Leusse.

The Role of Multinational Companies in Latin America

A Case Study in Mexico

REMY MONTAVON
with the collaboration of
MIGUEL WIONCZEK
and
FRANCIS PIQUEREZ

Published in association with the EUROPEAN CENTRE FOR STUDY AND INFORMATION ON MULTINATIONAL CORPORATIONS (ECSIM)
by
SAXON HOUSE, TEAKFIELD LIMITED
Westmead, Farnborough, Hampshire, England.

ISBN 0 566 00224 8.

Typeset by Inforum Ltd, Portsmouth
Printed in Great Britain by Biddles Ltd, Guildford

Contents

Preface   vii

PART I

1 SOCIO-ECONOMIC OVERVIEW OF MEXICO, 1960-75   3
   Evolution of the Economic Situation   3
   Evolution of the Social Situation   9

2 FOREIGN INVESTMENTS AND GOVERNMENT
     REGULATIONS   13
   Importance of Foreign Investments   13

PART II

   CASE STUDY: THE 'DANONE MEXICO' CORPORATION
   'A Joint Venture in the Mexican Food Industry'

3 THE MEXICAN FOOD INDUSTRY   23
   Structure   23
   Foreign Investments   25
   Overview of Food Industry Technology   28

4 THE DANONE MEXICO CORPORATION   30
   Introduction   30
   The Activities of Danone Mexico   37
   Economic Implications of the Presence in Mexico of
     BSN-Gervais Danone   52

PART III

   CASE STUDY: THE 'FIBRAS QUIMICAS SA'
     CORPORATION
   An Association between a Mexican Corporation, CYDSA SA, and
     a Dutch Corporation, AKZO, for the Production of Artificial
     and Synthetic Fibres

5 THE MEXICAN ARTIFICIAL AND SYNTHETIC FIBRE
     INDUSTRY   65
   Mexican Definition of the Chemical Industry and the
     Petrochemical Industry   65

The Petrochemical Industry   65
The Chemical Industry   68
The Artificial and Synthetic Fibre Industry   70
Integration of the Artificial and Synthetic Fibre
   Industry into the Petrochemical Industry   71

6 THE FIBRAS QUIMICAS SA CORPORATION   74
   Introduction: AKZO NV, The Dutch Mother Company   74
   The Mexican Group CYDSA SA, AKZO's Majority Partner (60%)
      in Fibras Quimicas SA Association and Technical Assistance
      Contract Between Fibras Quimicas and the AKZO GROUP   85
   Production   85
   Sales, results and financial situation   87
   Employment conditions   89
   Labour productivity   92
   The Mexican synthetic fibre market   93
   Technology transfer   95
   Taxes   97
   Balance of payments effects   98
   Some remarks   100

7 CONCLUSIONS   103
   Mexican Development Policy and the Activities of the Two Firms
   Studied   105
   Second Phase: The Promotion of a National Technology   106
   Third Phase: Regulation of Foreign Investments   108

SOURCES AND SUMMARY BIBLIOGRAPHY   112

Preface

The presence and operations of multinational corporations in the developing countries are frequently criticised; more even than in the industrial countries, where these corporations operate alongside structured national sectors and in the presence of 'counter-powers' which keep them under observation and occasionally attack them. It is usually admitted that the multinationals wield a decisive influence in a number of developing countries, certainly in the economic field.

This raises fundamental questions: do multinational corporations constitute a factor of economic autonomy or dependency as far as these countries are concerned? Do they or do they not promote economic integration in these countries? Do they meet the development priorities which these countries have selected?

The European Centre for Study and Information on Multinational Corporations aims to contribute to the improvement of knowledge of the way in which multinational corporations and society, in the broadest meaning of the term, interact. In this context, since its inception in 1976, it has selected as one of its principal lines of research analysis of the activities and impact of multinationals in the developing countries.

Although there was already a wide range of literature on the subject of multinationals, there seemed to be a gap as far as direct coverage and analysis of their operations was concerned. This being so, the ECSIM decided to initiate a thorough study of the effect which the operations of a limited number of firms have had in specific countries. To start with two countries were selected: Mexico and the Ivory Coast. Others will follow.

This methodology, which the ECSIM adopted after consultation with a group of experts,[1] offers the advantage of providing factual and detailed information which was previously little known or ignored. But it has a limitation in that it renders any generalisation about the overall impact of multinationals fairly hazardous.

In the case of the Ivory Coast,[2] the representative nature of the corporations studied, and the size and degree of industrialisation of the country, allowed for assessment of the global impact which the influx of foreign capital had had on the Ivory Coast economy, thanks to analysis of the operations and repercussions of three firms; whereas the same was not possible in the present study.

To achieve similar results for Mexico, an entirely different approach and far more substantial resources would have been necessary, owing to the vast size of the country and the extent to which multinationals have penetrated the Mexican economy.

Why then select Mexico at all? Because, since 1972, this important Latin American country has been pursuing a coherent policy of economic development; because, moreover, the government has created a system of industrial and technological policy instruments which clearly outline the fields in which foreign companies may operate, in order to allow for 'peaceful co-existence' between Mexican private or public enterprises and the multinational corporations.

The next step was to find European multinationals which were prepared to cooperate in implementing the project. Of the various corporations approached, only two, AKZO and BSN-Gervais Danone, agreed to open their books for this exercise. Thanks to their co-operation the authors of the study were able not only to analyse the reasons which caused them to start operating in Mexico as well as the nature of these operations, but also to evaluate the effect their presence had had on employment, on the distribution of incomes and on the balance of payments. In addition, an analysis was made of the nature, the machinery and the cost of transfers of technology by the parent companies to their subsidiaries.

In order to allow for analysis in greater depth and in order to introduce a factor for comparison, the national sector corresponding to the field of the two multinationals concerned has also been described briefly, i.e. the food industry as far as BSN-Gervais Danone is concerned, and the synthetic fibres industry as far as AKZO is concerned. In both cases, the study shows the share and the nature of the operations by foreign companies and by Mexican private or public companies.

To illustrate the context in which the multinationals concerned operate in the host country, the first part of the study consists of a socio-economic survey of Mexico from 1960 to 1975. It includes a chapter indicating the importance of foreign investors to the country's economy, and it describes the various laws and provisions which the government has introduced to regulate their activities.

In conclusion, the study sums up the trend of the development policy which Mexico has pursued, notably as regards industrialisation, the promotion of national technology, and regulation of foreign investments. In our opinion, this conclusion is interesting chiefly because it pinpoints, on the one hand, the framework and the area in which foreign investments operate, and on the other hand, the most obvious points to be covered in future negotiations between the political authorities and the multinational corporations.

What is clear is that the days when multinational corporations were able to operate without any constraints whatever are over. Their continued presence in the developing countries will be conditioned by their ability to adjust and to abide by the overall development objectives which governments have laid down.

ECSIM

Notes

[1] We are indebted to Jean Masini (University Paris I — IEDES), Sanjaya Lall (University of Oxford), Remy Montavon (Director of INDEVSA) and A.A.J. Van Bilsen (University of Ghent) who kindly gave us their help.

[2] *Multinationals and development in Black Africa: a case study in the Ivory Coast* by Jean Masini, Moises Ikonicoff, Claudio Jedlicki and Mario Lanzarotti.

PART I

1 Socio-Economic Overview of Mexico, 1960-75

Evolution of the economic situation

Economic growth

Of all the countries in Latin America, Mexico is the one whose economy experienced the highest and most regular growth rate during the period 1960 to 1975. This performance was even more noteworthy considering that until 1973, a year during which strong inflationary pressures began affecting the entire world, prices in Mexico had remained remarkably stable. Between 1960 and 1975, in fact, gross domestic product (GDP) growth maintained an average per annum growth rate in real terms of around 7 per cent, or roughly twice the rate of demographic growth (3.45 per cent). Thus, during those fifteen years, GDP increased, in real terms, by 160 per cent, going from 150,000 to 390.000 million pesos[1] (in 1960 pesos); per capita GDP grew by 55 per cent (in real terms and in 1960 pesos), from 4,310 to 6,600 pesos.

However, during the same period, growth rates taken not over a fifteen year average but in five-year increments showed a deceleration, caused by a series of structural obstacles proper to Mexico but also by the cyclical fluctuations of the world economy and its effects on Mexico. Thus, the average annual GDP growth of 7.2 per cent registered during 1961 to 1965 fell during the next five years to 6.9 per cent and in the period 1971 to 1975 fell even further to 5.6 per cent.

The importance given by Mexico, since the end of the 1930s, to industrialisation based on import substitution, provoked constant changes in the sectoral distribution of GDP in favour of the secondary sector. The proportion of this sector in GDP went, from 1960 to 1975, from 29.2 per cent to 35.7 per cent.

In 1973, the proportion of manufacturing industries in GDP was around 24 per cent. While in 1960 the greatest part of the sub-sector 'manufacturing industries' was producing consumer goods (largely non-durable), the decade between the early 1960s and the early 1970s witnessed the appearance in Mexico of a dynamic intermediate goods industry, a durable goods industry, and the beginnings of a capital goods industry.

The dynamic growth of the secondary sector, and particularly of the manufacturing industries, occurred at the expense of the primary sector whose proportion in GDP decreased from 15.9 per cent to 9.6 per cent between 1960 and 1975. The weakening of the primary sector brought to light two facts. First, the difficult situation in agriculture and the ever-widening gap between high-productivity commercial agriculture in the north and north-west of Mexico and subsistence agriculture typical of the central and south-eastern regions. Secondly, the lack of importance given in the official development strategy to the exploitation of mineral resources, with the exception of petroleum. (The exploitation of petroleum represents a special case in that hydrocarbons are the country's principal source of energy; it is estimated that petroleum fulfils 90 per cent of the total energy demand in Mexico.)

It must also be noted that the proportion of the tertiary sector in GDP has remained practically unchanged in the last 15 years: 54.9 per cent in 1960 and 54.7 per cent in 1975. But, as in the agricultural sector, the tertiary sector which offers the most employment in the country is basically composed of two highly distinct sub-sectors: one, modern and located in urban areas close to industrial units, is characterised by capital-intensity and high productivity; the other is mainly composed of small enterprises providing services of the traditional type, and includes all domestic employees in the cities.

Industrialisation

The average rate of industrial growth, which went as high as 7.4 per cent p.a. between 1960 and 1975, was the result of a different pace of development in the three sub-sectors of the manufacturing industries: non-durable consumer goods, intermediate goods, and durable consumer goods. In the 1950s, the progressive reduction in levels of substitution in imports of non-durable goods, persistent inflation and the concentration of income, provoked a relatively slow growth in the non-durable consumer goods sub-sector and much more rapid growth in the intermediate goods industry.

These differences in patterns of growth brought about significant changes in the country's industrial structure. In 1950, the non-durable consumer goods industry represented 75.3 per cent of the total value of the manufacturing sector. Intermediate goods represented 15.4 per cent, and durable consumer goods, particularly in the automobile industry, 9.3 per cent. In 1960 these percentages were 65.8 per cent, 21.6 per cent, and 12.6 per cent, respectively.

As early as 1960, a series of factors gave the manufacturing sector the characteristics of a more advanced economy. These were the affluence of foreign investments and the development of the automobile and petrochemical industries. The demand for non-durable consumer goods continued to grow at a slow rate. The industrial structure of the country in 1975 was thus very different from 1960: the non-durable goods sub-sector, which was considerably modernised, represented, in 1975, 51.8 per cent of the total value of the manufacturing industries, while intermediate goods represented 29.1 per cent and durable consumer and capital goods 19 per cent of the total. However, it must be pointed out that these figures hide a very late start in the capital goods sub-sector which, in 1975, represented barely 5 per cent of the country's manufacturing production. It is, in fact, the durable consumer goods sub-sector (especially the automobile and household appliances industries) which has grown the most.

In summary, one can say that in 1975, the basic characteristics of Mexican industry were as follows:

1 A great inter-sectoral heterogeneity and an increasing concentration of production in large industrial units.
2 The predominance of foreign capital in the dynamic branches, particularly in intermediate and durable goods, with the exception of steel and petrochemicals.
3 The use of capital-intensive technologies requiring relatively little labour.
4 A high degree of dependence on foreign technology.

To give an idea of the level of industrial concentration in Mexico, it is enough to mention that in 1970, or 30 years after the start of an import-substitution policy, 0.5 per cent of the industrial establishments (in fact, large industry) controlled, according to the 1970 census, almost 30 per cent of the invested capital and 24 per cent of the increase in value in the manufacturing sector. On the other hand, if one considers the 230 branches which make up the total of the manufacturing sector, one notes that in 46 of those branches, the 4 largest enterprises supplied 75 per cent of the production. In each of these branches, the 4 largest establishments produced, on the average, 46 per cent of the industrial output. As we might expect, the concentration level was even higher in the branches controlled by foreign capital.

The degree of concentration of industrial production is also very high geographically. In 1970, 75 per cent of industrial GDP was generated in only 8 administrative units which represented 49 per cent of the total population and 58 per cent of the urban population. Three of them, the Federal District, the States of Mexico and Nuevo Leon, which had 22.5 per cent of the total and 34.4 per cent of the urban populations, supplied 54 per cent of the gross industrial product; in fact, the Metropolitan region of Mexico City itself accounted for 45 per cent. Geographical concentration was of course much higher in 1970 than in 1940.

Investments

The total rate of investments in Mexico is still very high compared with the majority of Latin American countries; it remains in the neighbourhood of 20 per cent of GDP. Until 1970, private investments accounted for slightly less than 60 per cent with respect to slightly over 40 per cent for public sector investments. There have been important changes over the last few years, notably a decrease in the percentage of private investments due to the world economic recession of 1973 to 1975 and to the slow expansion of the domestic market, caused by a very high concentration of incomes. Moreover, the importance given by the State, starting in 1970, to social investments and to the expansion of anti-cyclical public expenditures, between 1973 and 1975, resulted in the fact that in 1975, for the first time in the history of Mexico, public sector investments were slightly higher than those of the private sector. While between 1971 and 1975 private investments grew at barely 1.3 per cent annually in constant prices, public investments recorded an average annual growth rate of 13.8 per cent.

Given the weakness of the foundations of the Mexican fiscal system, this recent growth in expenditures (particularly public sector investments) has had various effects on the economy. On the one hand, it has allowed the expansion and the upgrading of the country's infrastructure and the quality of social services, and for the gradual (yet insufficient) growth of employment; on the other hand, it has triggered off an acceleration in the inflation rate, a considerable increase in public spending deficit, and deficits in the balance of trade and in the balance of payments which have had to be almost entirely compensated for by new public sector borrowing from foreign sources of capital.

During the last 15 years, the breakdown in public investments between investments of a social nature and investments for the industrial sector has changed considerably. While until 1965, about 68 per cent of investments by the public sector were going into industry, communications and transport, those going into agriculture and social services represented only a little more than 25 per cent. Starting in 1970, those last two sectors received priority at the expense of industry, communications and transport. From 1973 to 1975, over half of public investments went into agriculture and social services. Let us keep in mind that in Mexico, public expenditures for administrative services and defence are very low and never more than 5 per cent of total public investments.

Fiscal policy and public finances

According to the development strategy adopted during the Second World War, the Mexican governments continued, during the 1960s, to follow a fiscal policy which favoured productive activities, national as well as foreign, in the private sector. In addition to a relatively low fiscal load, this policy included incentives and fiscal exemptions for private industry and called for high public expenditures in infrastructure and in those basic industries necessary to ensure the profitability of private investments.

The continued growth of federal expenditures, the relative stability of tax income as a percentage of GDP, the somewhat poor financial performance of a number of nationalised industries — all these factors resulted in a constant increase in the public sector deficit. For the Federal government this deficit, which had been around 20 per cent from 1965 to 1970, went up to nearly 30 per cent from 1971 to 1975. Until 1972, this growing deficit was compensated for by national private savings, by blocking an ever larger proportion of bank deposits in the Central Bank, and by borrowing from outside; and starting in 1973, by injecting money more and more frequently into the economy. These last measures, coinciding with foreign inflationary pressures on imports, are partly responsible for the reappearance of a very high rate of inflation beginning in

1974 — a rate which remains uncontrolled to this day and which was further stimulated by the devaluation of the peso at the end of 1976.

Price stability and inflation

During the postwar period, the Mexican economy suffered from inflation for the first time between 1945 and 1960. During this time, the average annual rate of increase in wholesale prices was 6.4 per cent. Inflation was controlled in the 1960s and that rate was brought back down to 2.5 per cent. Various factors made this result possible, namely an abundant domestic supply of food products, subsidies for energy costs, the relatively low cost of foreign loans made by the State, and finally, a policy of low wages throughout industry. This remarkable price stability was interrupted in the early 1970s. The average annual increase in inflation, between 1970 and 1975 was 10 per cent between 1974 and 1975, it passed 20 per cent and in 1976 reached around 30 per cent, largely because of the devaluation which took place on 1 September. The rate of inflation would have been even higher if the State, thanks to its political control over the organised labour unions, had not succeeded in slowing down salary increases which, in real terms, have declined by at least 25 per cent between 1974 and 1976. This wage policy would not have been possible if the country had not experienced growing unemployment and under-employment, worsened by the arrival of ever-increasing manpower on the job market. This situation can also partly explain the absence, to this day, of widespread strike movements.

Balance of payments and foreign trade

Despite the good performance of the Mexican economy, its balance of payments situation is no different from that of other developing countries, with imports of goods and services far higher than exports. This current account deficit is compensated for by the inflow of capital, direct private foreign investments as well as loans largely destined to the public sector. Tourist income, especially from North America, and remittances by Mexicans working in the United States, play an equally positive role in the balance of payments. Until the end of the 1960s, the balance of payments deficit was of reasonable size: $167.2 million in 1960 and $300 million in 1965. The situation began to get worse beginning in the early 1970s, because of various factors; increases in import prices for intermediary and capital goods, stagnation in agricultural production of food products destined for domestic consumption, a decrease in competitiveness of export products, and finally, the rapid increase in the expenditures of Mexican tourists abroad.

Between 1970 and 1975, Mexican exports of goods and services increased by only 100 per cent (this increase corresponding almost entirely to the increases in international prices), going from $3.1 to $6.3 billion.[2] Imports, on the other hand, went up 150 per cent in the same period from $4 to $10.1 billion. The corresponding deficit was only partly covered by inflows of private foreign capital, the balance by increased foreign borrowing. As a result, the country's public foreign debt went up from $7 billion in 1970 to $20.3 billion at the end of 1975. A greater part of this new foreign debt corresponds to Euro-currency credits which amounted, between 1971 and 1975, to $5.8 billion, i.e. more than 30 per cent of all the credits from the Euro-market destined to Latin American countries. It is worth noting here that the servicing of this public foreign debt absorbs 25 per cent of the value of Mexican exports of goods and services.

Between 1960 and 1975, the structure of exports and imports underwent a radical change, because of the country's industrialisation and its growing difficulties in the agricultural sector. In 1960, 52 per cent of exports came from the agricultural sector and consisted of non-transformable products and raw materials, 21 per cent came from the extractive industries, of which 18.6 per cent from the mining sector and 2.7 per cent from petroleum. Only 18.3 per cent of the total came from exports of manufactured goods — from the food, textile and chemical industries.

The picture in 1975 was totally different. The amount of the agricultural sector in exports had gone down to 20.8 per cent. Extractive industries had increased to 25.8 per cent, despite a relative decrease in the mining sector which was compensated for by larger petroleum exports. But the exports of manufactured products were the most dynamic, reaching 42 per cent in 1975 as against 18.3 per cent 15 years earlier. The rate of expansion of manufactured goods had accelerated the most between 1970 and 1975. Their greater diversification is also noteworthy; traditional exports (food, textiles and chemicals) increased by only 2.9 per cent, the others by 17.1 per cent. If we add the assembly plants ('maquiladores') on the US border, we notice that in fact the exports of manufactured goods represented in 1975 half the country's total exports.

The structure of imports shows a relative decrease in the imports of consumer goods; 17.9 per cent and 19.9 per cent for 1960 and 1970 respectively, as against 9.1 per cent of the total in 1975. Such encouraging results should be cautiously examined, however. In fact, official import statistics include a list of categories of non-classified products, of which most are consumer goods: they represent 10.4 per cent of the total. In addition, and for obvious reasons, these figures do not take into account smuggling, which is always in consumer goods. Finally, 1975 having been a year of economic recession, it cannot be considered as typical. It is thus difficult to maintain that the structure of imports has clearly improved in the last 15 years because of the country's progress in industrialisation. Pressures on imports come from different sources; stagnation in the agricultural sector, an out-of-proportion level of industrial protection, the failure to integrate the industrial structure, and the concentration of incomes.

The rare available statistics seem to show that the highest growth in exports of manufactured goods comes from foreign companies located in Mexico. While the percentage of exports of industrial production was 2.6 per cent in 1972, foreign industries and industries under foreign control exported, that same year, 2.8 per cent of their production. But it is evident that in either case, more than 95 per cent of industrial production was destined for the domestic market. For imports, the situation is different. For the total of the manufacturing industry, the import coefficient is 5.1 per cent, and for foreign firms it is close to 12 per cent, which shows that the durable consumer goods industry and the capital goods industry are still very dependent on the imports of spare parts and equipment. The import coefficient of foreign firms is not above 3 per cent in the non-durable consumer goods industries; it is 13 per cent in the chemical industry, 16 per cent in the electrical equipment industry and 23 per cent in the automobile industry.

Evolution of the social situation

Population and employment

Over the last twenty-five years, the population of Mexico had an annual rate of growth of 3.45 per cent and life expectancy went from 58.9 years in 1960 to 62.1 years in 1970. Thus, total population went from 34.9 million in 1960 to 48.2 million in 1970 and over 59 million in 1975. The rate of population growth, however, has shown a slight decrease — to 3.25 per cent in 1975.

Two specific phenomena accompanied this explosive population growth, large migrations both within the country and to the USA, and extremely rapid urbanisation. Between 1960 and 1970 (date of the last census) urban (i.e. over 2,500 inhabitants) population grew from 17.7 to 28.3 million, or from 50.7 per cent to 58.7 per cent of the total. In absolute terms, rural population has grown as well — from 18.7 to 19.9 million during the same period — yet its percentage of the total dropped from 49.3 per cent to 41.3 per cent, again reflecting the urbanisation trend.

The active population, defined in Mexico as all persons over twelve years of age excepting students, was estimated at 11.25 million in 1960 and 13 million in 1970. In 1960, over half the active population worked in agriculture, livestock breeding and connected activities. By 1970, this sector employed only around 5.1 million. Industry, the second most important sector in terms of employment, accounted for 2.2 million in 1960 and nearly 3 million in 1970. The service sector absorbs the greatest portion of young people joining the active population.

There are no reliable statistics in Mexico on unemployment and under-employment. According to the 1960 census, there were 182,000 unemployed (i.e. 1.6 per cent of the active population). By 1970, the number of unemployed had grown to 485,000 (or 3.75 per cent of the active population). But clearly, these figures do not take into account under-employment, particularly in the agricultural and service sectors, and also apparently do not estimate correctly the amount

9

of unemployment. According to recent data received at the Labour Ministry, 9 per cent of the active population was unemployed at the beginning of 1977, and under-employment was estimated at 40 per cent. Perhaps these figures over estimate under-employment and structural unemployment. The country's best economists situate unemployment at around 7 per cent of the active population (for 1970 to 1975), plus an under-employment factor of around 25 per cent.

For a long time it was thought in Mexico that accelerated industrialisation would resolve the unemployment problem. The 1975 industrial census confirms the doubts which had been expressed recently concerning that hypothesis. Preliminary analyses indicate the rate of absorption of labour by industry had in fact decreased between 1970 and 1975. New job openings in industry, which had gone up 18 per cent between 1965 and 1970, dropped to 10.4 per cent between 1970 and 1975. This phenomenon was no doubt caused by technological progress and by the absorption of small and medium sized enterprises into larger and more modern units. In a number of industrial branches, notably in the production of non-durable consumer goods, even the absolute number of jobs decreased during those last five years. This happened in the tobacco, textile, shoe, leather and graphic industries.

Distribution of national income

Even though *per capita* income tripled, in constant prices, between 1950 and 1970, there is a lack of detailed studies on the distribution of that income. According to an American economist[3] national income distribution in 1968 was as follows (population being divided into four social classes in decreasing order of income):

Class A: 10% of the population; 37% of national income
Class B: 40% of the population; 37% of national income
Class C: 40% of the population; 22% of national income
Class D: 10% of the population; 4% of national income.

This inequality in income distribution is more pronounced in Mexico than in any other Latin American country except Brazil, where in 1975 the top 10 per cent had 46 per cent of the national income while the bottom 10 per cent disposed of 1 per cent.

Partial studies indicate that some progress took place between 1950 and 1970. For instance, the 5 per cent richest families had 36 per cent of the national income in 1969 as against 40.8 per cent in 1950. For the same period, the bottom half of the social classes saw its share decrease from 19 per cent to 15 per cent, while the intermediate group went up from 40.2 per cent to 49 per cent. These figures reflect the regular expansion of the urban middle classes and the relative impoverishment of the classes with the lowest resources. On an absolute scale, however, real income has increased for all social classes, but for the poor at a slower rate than for the middle classes. Many observers have said that half the Mexican families do not really live, they merely survive.

What is certain is that an increasing rate of growth of inflation during recent years has exacerbated the inequalities in income distribution. It should be noted, however, to get a fair idea of the current situation in Mexico, that the poorest populations have also benefited, both qualitatively and quantitatively, from the expansion of public social services particularly in education, housing and health.

Education

Half the country's population is under fifteen years of age and the school-age population (between five and twenty-four) went from 16.2 million to 26.9 million between 1960 and 1975. These figures illustrate the difficult situation in which the country's educational system finds itself. The figures also show why, despite enormous progress during the last ten years, the system has not been able to satisfy the demand in the school-age range. The future of Mexico is being heavily mortgaged by this inability to fully prepare human resources.

The development and improvement of educational infrastructure have been significant and public expenditures for education have increased more rapidly than for other sectors. The Education Ministry's budget quadrupled between 1970 and 1975, from 8 billion to 30.7 billion pesos.

Primary school registrations grew at an annual rate of 5.9 per cent over the last twenty-five years. For secondary schools, the rate has been 14.3 per cent. For advanced-level schooling, the rate has been 11.6 per cent; between 1970 and 1975, the rates have been even higher. The total in all educational categories went up by 38 per cent, from 11.5 to 15.9 million students. Despite these positive results, in 1974 some 20 per cent of the population between six and fourteen years of age was not registered in primary school, and 60 per cent in the fifteen to nineteen year range were not registered in secondary schools. Under these conditions, and especially with its overall population growth rate, Mexico is still far from being able to give a primary school education to all its children under fourteen years of age, or a secondary education to the majority of its adolescents. It has been impossible to eliminate illiteracy (6.1 million people in 1975), or to reduce the number of functional illiterates. Neither have increased expenditures eliminated the very marked differences in educational levels between regions; the industrially under-developed States are also the ones with the lowest educational levels.

It should be underlined that technical education at the middle level, which had developed slowly until 1970 has increased considerably in recent years. In this type of school, registrations have gone from 35,000 to 80,000 to 240,000 in 1950, 1960 and 1970, respectively. Between 1970 and 1975, more than 800 middle-level technical schools were created, with an enrolment of 530,000 students. But this figure represents only 30 per cent of the total registrations in secondary schools and seems insufficient to ensure the country's future technical development.

Advanced-level schooling registrations increased by 15 per cent annually starting in 1970. Only 25,000 university students were registered in the country in 1950. By the end of 1975, this number had grown to 442,000, representing 3.6 per cent of all students and 20 per cent of the national budget for education.

Post-graduate education is still very limited because of lack of planning in the various disciplines, the concentration of all such institutions in the capital and the small number of professors qualified for that sort of teaching. In 1967, there were 2,200 post-graduate students, by 1970 the number had grown to 5,800 and reached about 10,000 by the end of 1975.

Housing

As in other developing countries, the housing problem is far from being resolved. In 1970, it was estimated that to satisfy the needs of homeless families, or to replace or repair sub-standard housing as well as reduce the number of inhabitants per unit, some 5.1 million units would have to be built.

This situation resulted principally from the State's near total lack of participation in housing construction, at least up to 1970. It has been estimated that between 1960 and 1970, less than 5 per cent of public expenditures for construction were for social purposes. During the same period, 90 per cent of private investment in this sector was used to finance middle class and upper class housing, and practically all in the large cities.

It was only after the 1968 outbursts that the State changed its policy. In 1970, public expenditures for low-cost housing were four times what they had been in 1960. They doubled between 1970 and 1974, reaching 20 per cent of public expenditure for construction compared to 5 per cent during the 1960s. Thus, the ratio of public to private sector construction financing, which had been 1:10 in the 1960s, went to 1:2 by the end of 1975. This new social, low-cost housing was built not only in the largest cities but also throughout the country in smaller towns.

Notes

[1] From 1960 to 1975, fixed parity between the Mexican peso and the US dollar was 12.5.
[2] 1 billion = 1,000,000,000
[3] Clark W. Reynolds, *The Mexican Economy: Twentieth Century Structure and Growth.*

2 Foreign Investments and Government Regulations

Importance of foreign investments

Private foreign investments have increased with regularity over the past 25 years. At the end of 1973, their value was estimated at $3.7 billion, of which 76.5 per cent was of US origin. A Mexican policy aiming at diversifying the sources of foreign investments has met with only limited success. The European countries — by order of importance; West Germany, UK, Switzerland, Sweden, Italy, France and the Netherlands — were in second place with $654 million, or 17.8 per cent of the total.

Because of the growing interest of European firms to establish themselves in Mexico, the percentage of US investments decreased somewhat and was roughly 75 per cent of the total in 1975, as against 80 per cent five years earlier. The percentage of European investments grew proportionately. The sectoral breakdown of these investments shows that the interest of foreign firms was highest in the industrial sector, with 75.5 per cent of the total in 1973, followed by trade with 14.8 per cent and mining with 5.4 per cent. Foreign investments in agriculture, construction, electricity production and communications were negligible.

Despite the official 'Mexicanisation' policy, majority control is still in foreign hands in the majority of firms with foreign participation, i.e. joint ventures. At the end of 1975, out of 4,083 joint ventures, 64.2 per cent were under foreign control, 27.3 per cent had a foreign participation between 25 per cent and 49.9 per cent, and in only 8.5 per cent of the firms was foreign control less than 25 per cent of the capital. In the transformation industries, where foreign investments are the highest, the percentages of foreign control were slightly higher than the averages given above.

Data from the US Department of Commerce tell us that the average annual growth rate of direct private investments in Mexico was 8.4 per cent from 1961 to 1965, 9.3 per cent from 1966 to 1970, and 12.2 per cent from 1971 to 1974, with the highest relative growth rates in the trade and manufacturing sectors. On the other hand, investments in the mining, foundry, petroleum and public service industries decreased in relative as well as absolute terms between 1960 and 1974.

Although detailed official information concerning the sources of new investments, the final destination of profits and the payments of royalties and interest is not available for the period after 1965, we do know that the total of these outflows is higher than the sum of new investments and re-investments of profits by foreign investors. We also know that a good portion of new investments is in fact composed of re-investments of profits.

13

Profitability of US investments in Mexico, net of local taxes, had also continued to increase. It was 6.8 per cent of book value in 1960, 7.9 per cent in 1970, and 12.6 per cent in 1974. These figures do not include payments made abroad for interest, royalties or technical assistance. These categories of payments have grown more rapidly in recent years than profits.

The Law of May, 1973, on foreign investments: first experiences

Foreign investment policy has been regulated since May, 1973, by the 'Law for the Promotion of Mexican Investments and the Regulation of Foreign Investments'. This Law gathers together and applies the legislations in force since 1944 and regulates foreign investment in most economic activities.

According to this Law, foreign investors who wish to engage in joint ventures in Mexico are welcome, particularly those who bring labour-intensive technologies, who contribute to the geographical decentralisation of the economy; who will have a favourable effect on the balance of payments and who will integrate into their production the largest amount of local raw materials, and finally, who will not reduce the local sources of credit for local firms and who will not impose patterns of consumption judged to be useless.

Certain economic activities are the preserve of the State: petroleum and other hydrocarbons, the exploitation of radioactive minerals and the production of nuclear energy, mines, electricity, railways and telegraphic and radio communications.

Reserved for Mexicans or Mexican firms, without any foreign participation, are radio and television, urban and interurban transport services, aerial and maritime transport, exploitation of forests and gas distribution.

Foreign investors can participate in the following economic activities, according to a fixed percentage: exploitation and use of minerals subject to regular concessions up to a maximum of 49 per cent, and in the case of special concessions for minerals judged to be of national interest, up to 34 per cent, secondary products of the petrochemical industry, up to 40 per cent, and manufacture of spare parts for the automotive industry, up to 40 per cent. In all other cases, foreign participation is allowed up to 49 per cent, but not if the effective control of such a joint venture would be in foreign hands.

In order to create the controls necessary for the application of the new Law, two new governmental organisations were created, the National Committee for Foreign Investments and the National Registry for Foreign Investments. The National Committee deals with all the cases which might not have been foreseen by the Law, and gives or refuses its approval to all future requests for either an increase or a decrease in participation as specified in the Law. It also determines the conditions which have to be fulfilled for any new investment or for any re-investment of profits by firms wishing to enter a new field of activity.

At the end of 1975, the National Register featured 4,083 firms having part of their capital under foreign control. Within this total, 2,105 (or slightly over one-half) were in the manufacturing sector and represented 75 per cent of foreign investment in Mexico. Of the remainder, 919 were involved in trade, 771 in the service sector, and the others were spread out over various sectors.

It is still too early to draw conclusions on the consequences of the application of the Law of 1973. However, some effects can already be identified. Data obtained from the National Committee show that foreign firms have quickly adapted themselves to the conditions of minority participation defined in the Law, and there have been only a few exceptional demands by foreign firms to gain majority control. Of 345 new joint ventures created since the Law went into effect, 338 followed the Law's stipulations without requesting an exemption. The National Committee authorised majority control only in cases where the foreign investor was able to prove that this would result in important economic benefits to the country. In the few rare instances where the National Committee refused a request or imposed severe restrictions, the firms concerned were in the fields of internal trade, real estate or advertising.

Another indirect effect of the Law has shown itself in the diversification of investment sources; of the twenty-eight joint ventures created between 1973 and 1976 with a capital over 10 million pesos, fourteen resulted from a partnership agreement between public or private Mexican firms and foreign firms from Japan, West Germany, Switzerland, France and Italy. In addition, the Law put an end to the practice of acquiring majority control in firms which had previously been entirely Mexican. One should bear in mind that between 1958 and 1967, 66 per cent of foreign investments were effected simply by foreigners buying shares in Mexican firms.

Finally the Law has not stopped, let alone slowed down, the flow of foreign investment. On the contrary, while in 1972 direct foreign investments were estimated at 2.4 billion pesos, they grew to 3.4 billion in 1973, 4.5 billion in 1974 and about 5 billion in 1975.

Regulations on technology transfers

Towards the end of the 1960s, a new trend of opinion took over governmental, academic and even business circles. As a result of concerns expressed over the magnitude of outflows of hard currencies for royalties and technical assistance fees, and other numerous restrictions imposed by the owners of imported technologies on their uses, the government enacted the 1972 Law on 'Technology Transfers and the Use of Patents and Trademarks'.

The Law basically aimed at the following objectives:

1 To regulate technology transfers in such a way that contract terms would correspond to the socio-economic development objectives of the country and would ensure national independence;

2 To reinforce the negotiating power of buyers of technology and ensure fav-

ourable contract terms;

3 To make Mexican industrialists more conscious of the need for a rapid diffusion and assimilation of technology within the country to encourage its development; and

4 To establish an offical registry where contract terms and the problems inherent in technology transfers might be more easily accessible, in order to define better the conditions for the industrial and technological development of the country.

The Law provides for fourteen cases where registration must be refused. These cases can be grouped under four general headings:

1 When the asking price or compensatory offer is out of line with the value of the technology to be acquired, or else represents too heavy a load on the national economy;

2 Where the judicial base for future arbitration of conflicts or varying contractual interpretations is located outside of Mexico;

3 Where the length of the contract is considered excessive and, in any case, when it surpasses 10 years; and

4 When the contract contains restrictive clauses concerning exports, production and sales; the utilisation of complementary technologies, research, administration, or the purchase of raw materials or industrial machinery and equipment.

By March 31st, 1976, requests for registration were made for 5,087 contracts. In 605 cases, the request was refused. In order of importance, the reasons for rejection were as follows: a price out of line with the value of the imported technology or a price exceeding international averages for the same technology, a length of contract judged to be excessive, limitations to the production scale, and in last place, the choice of a judicial base outside of Mexico.

Before registration, all contracts are subjected to an economic, technical and legal analysis to determine if the conditions of purchase of the foreign technology are in harmony with the interests of the buyer and of the national economy. On the other hand, the technical content of the contracts is not analysed. A large number of contracts were renegotiated between 1973 and 1976 before being resubmitted to the Committee. A large number of restrictive clauses were eliminated through this process, and it is estimated that savings of up to 4.6 billion pesos were realised during that period.

Mexican policies concerning industrial property

Mexican policies in this area are directly relevant to foreign firms; in fact, in the majority of cases, the firms establishing themselves in Mexico are motivated by a desire to further exploit brand names and patents which have already proved themselves in industrialised countries.

The Law on Inventions and Trademarks went into effect in February, 1976, complementing the Law of May, 1973 on foreign investments and superceding the legal norms established in 1942. The new Law regulates invention patents and their subsequent improvements, industrial designs and mock-ups, and the use of foreign brand names. It also sets up new standards and norms to fight against illegal competition in the use of brands and inventions.

Without going into extensive details, we can cite the following clauses of the Law of 1976 bearing on policies of joint ventures or foreign firms:

1 The Law protects all inventions or patents up to 10 years only, as opposed to 15 years previously;
2 The Law excludes concessions of patents for inventions having to do with health, agricultural production, environmental protection and nuclear energy. Thus, manufacturing processes for chemicals and pharmaceuticals, medicines, beverages, fertilisers, insecticides and herbicides cannot be patented; however, certificates of invention can be granted to the holders of patents for such manufacturing processes, affording them some protection. But this certificate does not grant exclusive rights to its holder. Rather, anyone can use the patent conditional upon payment of a royalty whose amount has to be submitted for approval to the Committee of the National Registry for Technology Transfers;
3 The Law grants protection for trademarks for a period of 5 years, as against 10 previously. When a copyright is held by a foreigner or already registered abroad, it must also be associated with a copyright in Mexico. In such a case, the Mexican brand name must be as visible on the product as the foreign brand name.

Thus, the measures taken by the Mexican government beginning in 1972 resulted in a set of instruments with which to apply a more coherent industrialisation policy than in the past. In the debates and written works dealing with the influence of multinational firms established in developing countries, the fact that the host countries should carefully delimit what those subsidiaries can and cannot do, is often mentioned. Mexico is thus one of the rare examples where the rules of the game have been carefully spelt out.

Could we conceive of even more rigorous legislation on the part of developing countries? In the final analysis, and no matter what the legislation, everything really depends on its application and on the economic and financial 'health' of the host country.

The various measures taken in Mexico are recent and even though MNC subsidiaries have already been subject to a great number of studies, to our knowledge there have, as yet, been no case studies of MNC affiliates or subsidiaries established in the country, written in the light of the new legislation. Moreover, the problems that Mexico is experiencing because of the pesos's 1976 devaluation would make such studies tentative at best. Our two case studies may be interesting in this regard. One deals with the company Danone Mexico which produces yogurts and prepared sweets. This is an affiliate of the French Group BSN-Gervais Danone. The other concerns Fibras Quimicas producing synthetic fibres, which is an affiliate of the Dutch AKZO.

The following Tables summarise various aspects of foreign investments in Mexico as well as some relevant data on the Mexican economy.

Table 2.1

Mexico — Gross Domestic Product
(in millions of pesos)

Years	In current prices	Percentage increase	In 1960 prices	Percentage increase	Average annual rate (%)
1960	150,511	—	150,511	—	
1961	163,265	8.5	157,931	4.9	
1962	176,030	7.8	165,310	4.7	
1963	195,983	11.3	178,516	8.0	1961-65
1964	231,370	18.1	199,390	11.7	7.2
1965	252,028	8.9	212,320	6.5	
1966	280,090	11.1	227,037	6.9	
1967	306,317	9.4	241,272	6.3	
1968	339,145	10.7	260,901	8.1	1966-70
1969	374,900	10.5	277,400	6.3	6.9
1970	418,700	11.7	296,600	6.9	
1971	452,400	8.0	306,800	3.4	
1972	512,300	13.2	329,100	7.3	
1973	619,600	20.9	354,100	7.6	1971-75
1974	813,700	31.3	375,000	5.9	5.6
1975	987,700	21.4	390,900	4.2	

Source: Banco de Mexico SA, *Annual Report, 1975*, Mexico, 1976, p. 63.

18

Table 2.2

Private Foreign Investments in Mexico
Distribution by Country
(in millions of US $)

	1970	1971	%	1972	%	1973*	%	1974
United States		2,425	80.9	2,537	79.9	2,800	76.5	
Canada		52		66		80		
West Germany		83		96		154		
United Kingdom		89		121		149		
Switzerland		84		76		140		
Sweden	Europe	37	14.3	45	14.9	63	17.9	
Italy		49		52		57		
France		50		46		47		
Netherlands		37		37		44		
Venezuela		7		7		6		
Japan		22		38		58		
Others		62		53		60		
Total		2,997	100	3,174	100	3,658	100	

* Preliminary figures.
Source: Banco de Mexico, S. Amin: *American Chamber of Commerce of Mexico A.C* The Influence of Direct Private Foreign Investments on the Mexican Economy. January, 1976, page 69.

Table 2.3

Sectoral Distribution of Foreign
Investments in Mexico
(in millions of US $)

Sectors	Years 1971	1972	1973
Agriculture	35	40	45
Mining	134	151	197
Petroleum	7	8	8
Industry	2,254	2,377	2,769
Construction	7	5	6
Electricity	3	3	3
Trade	474	515	541
Transport and Communications	8	10	10
Others	75	65	79
Total	2,997	3,174	3,658

Source: same as for Table 2.2

Table 2.4

Direct United States Investments in Mexico
(in millions of US $)

Years	Accumulated investments	Average annual rate of growth %	Profits	Profitability (percentage of investment)
1960	795	—	54	6.8
1965	1182	(1961-1965) 8.4	96	8.1
1970	1786	(1966-1970) 9.3	141	7.9
1974	2825	(1972-1974) 15.5	355	12.6

Source: 'Survey of Current Business' US Department of Commerce, 1955-1975, published in: *American Chamber of Commerce of Mexico, A.C.;* idem., Table I, page 210.

Table 2.5

Joint Ventures in Mexico
Percentage of Foreign Participation and
Sectoral Distribution — End 1975

Sector	No. of firms	Foreign Participation				Total %
		Up to 24.9%	25 to 49.9%	50%	50.1 to 100%	
Agriculture and livestock breeding	25	—	16.0	—	84.0	100
Extractive industries	243	8.2	79.0	—	12.8	100
Transformation industries	2,105	6.9	27.3	3.0	62.8	100
Trade	919	7.5	18.1	1.9	72.5	100
Transport	20	—	20.0	—	80.0	100
Services	771	14.3	22.6	1.3	61.8	100
Total	4,083	8.5	27.3	2.2	62.0	100

Source: General Direction of the 'National Registry for Foreign Investments'. Published in: Mauricio de Maria y Campos, *Policy and Results in the Matter of Foreign Investments*, Foreign Trade, Banco Nacional de Comercio Exterior, SA, vol. XVI, no. 7, Supplement, July 1976.

PART II

CASE STUDY: THE 'DANONE MEXICO' CORPORATION

A Joint Venture in the Mexican Food Industry

3 The Mexican Food Industry

In its factory established in 1973 in Huehuetoca, about 60 km. from Mexico City, the Danone Mexico Corporation produces yogurt and prepared desserts. The firm, a 49 per cent subsidiary of the French corporation BSN-Gervais Danone, is considered in Mexico as a medium-sized enterprise: in 1975 it had 100 employees and its annual turnover was 27 million pesos.

To appreciate the firm's activities it is important to have an overview of the structure of the Mexican food industry and of the importance of foreign investments in this sector. Contrary to the case study itself, this brief analysis is based on statistics and data from Mexican sources and foreign sources, and not from a field study of each of the companies covered. We have consulted different industrial data, the manufacturers' associations and the literature published on this topic, as well as various studies on foreign investments undertaken both in Mexico and in the United States. We should, therefore, consider these statistics with caution. They do not provide an analysis faithful in all respects to the food industry, but they do give a fairly good general approximation of the situation.

Structure

The food industry in general

The food industry is the most important industrial sector in the country. It represents, approximately, one seventh of gross investments in transformation industries, almost one fifth of the gross value of total industrial output, and if one excepts petroleum refining and primary and secondary petrochemcial industries, it is ranked fifth in industrial employment.

Official statistics divide the food industry into two large categories. The first comprises about 50,000 establishments of the family type which employ up to five people and produce, in a small-crafts way, food products based on wheat and corn (notably 'tortillas') as well as various simple foodstuffs destined for local consumption in the immediate vicinity of the production itself. The second category comprises about 8,400 firms which employ more than five people. The gross average value of annual production of each of the craft-like 50,000 establishments was in the order of 200,000 pesos in 1975 (about $16,000). Production averaged 1 million pesos for each of the 8,400 establishments in the second category.

These averages do not reveal very much about the structure of the food industry, in fact, of the 8,400 establishments in the second category, about 8,000 are of small and medium size while 400 are considered as large enterprises. Let us add that in 1970, four enterprises in this branch produced between themselves 21.5 per cent of the total output of the Mexican food industry.

This high degree of industrial concentration is less important than in the non-alcoholic beverage industry, where in 1970, four enterprises controlled 30 per cent of the national production.

As far as the recent evolution of the sector is concerned, one should note that rapid demographic growth and urbanisation in Mexico have provoked a large increase in the number of small and medium-sized enterprises which, between 1970 and 1975, went from 4,800 to 8,400. In that same period the value of total production, in current prices, doubled from 35,990 million to 78,670 million pesos (about 122 per cent), while in the same time the gross value added in the entire industry increased by 133 per cent. Because of automation, mechanisation and growing concentration of production in the large firms, job creation in the food industry progressed very slowly: in 1975 the 8,400 establishments with more than five employees occupied 228,600 people, while in 1970 the 4,800 enterprises in the same category had 202,000 employees. The relative increase in employment was thus about 13 per cent.

The high level of concentration which we have already mentioned can also be observed in the range of products and in the geographical location of factories. The 400 enterprises, which comprise the greater part of the food industry, produce more than 2,500 different articles which are registered with the health authorities and sold throughout the country. (Taking into account the different formats of these same articles, their number would come to about 3,700.) These 400 firms operate 500 plants. The 60 largest firms put on the market 10 basic products and operate 200 factories which produce 1,600 different articles. They work simultaneously in different product lines. For example, Elias Pando SA, a national food industry firm, has nine plants and produces almost 200 articles, thus occupying first place in product diversification. Second place goes to an American firm, Gerber Products SA, which in one single factory produces more than a hundred products for the feeding of babies and small children.

Large industry in the food sector is geographically located in large centres of consumption or in the agricultural and livestock-breeding zones of an industrial type. Sixty per cent of the 500 plants belonging to the 400 largest enterprises are located in the capital city or nearby, i.e. in the most industrialised part of the country. The following 20 per cent are established to the north of Baja California, in the states of Sinaloa and Jalisco (Guadalajara), as well as in the livestock-breeding and agricultural zones in the States of Guanajuato and Queretaro. Compared with that, regions in the south east and on the southern coast of the Pacific, which are essentially agricultural regions, have no food industry establishments with the exception of a Nestle factory in the state of Chiapas.

The milk products industry

The milk products industry is the most dynamic of all branches in the food industry. In 1975, it comprised 261 firms versus 271 in 1970, 223 in 1965 and 135 in 1960. Between 1960 and 1975 the value of gross output in current prices, went up fifteen-fold; between 1970 and 1975, the value of gross output tripled, from 3,900 million to 11,400 million pesos. Thus the milk products industry accounted for almost 15 per cent of the total output of the food industry in 1975, as against 7.6 per cent in 1960.

Despite the very large growth in production, employment in this branch only grew from 12,200 to 13,100 employees between 1960 and 1975. This only confirms that the basic Mexican policy of industrialisation without limits, based on import substitution, did not resolve the problem of labour absorption.

In the milk products industry, the sub-branch 'yogurt, desserts, and similar products', which are the main products of Danone Mexico, has a very limited scope. According to statistics and the industrial census, this sub-branch in 1970 comprised 29 establishments of more than five people for a gross production value of 119 million pesos and a total employment of 731 persons. By 1975, the number of firms had decreased by one, the total employed had grown by 287 persons, and the value of production had reached 316 million pesos. In terms of jobs, gross production, and value added, the contribution of this sub-branch to the total of the food industry represented only 0.35 per cent in 1970 and 0.4 per cent in 1975.

Later in the part of this study which deals specifically with Danone Mexico, we shall see what share the foreign and national firms hold in this market.

Foreign investments

In Mexican industry, the chemical sector draws the most foreign investments and the food sector comes in second place. According to the US Commerce Department, sales of foreign firms in the food sector established in Mexico represented, in 1974, 17 per cent of all the sales by foreign-controlled firms. According to another study,[1] Mexico is ranked fourth in the world after Canada, the United Kingdom, and West Germany in total turnover of American subsidiaries in the food industry.

The value of foreign investments in the food industry has increased rapidly during the past twenty years, from $20 million in 1950 to $63.4 million in 1960 and $235.5 million in 1970. This represents for those same years 13.4 per cent, 10.5 per cent, and 11.3 per cent, respectively, of all foreign investments. It is estimated that in 1975 this value was over $300 million. However, we must note that in recent years foreign investments have been directed more towards sectors with the highest growth rates, namely the electrical appliances and machinery industries and the transport industry.

In 1970, the food industry firms owned by foreigners employed 25,000 people, or 12.5 per cent of the jobs in food enterprises employing more than five people. By comparison, foreign firms in the chemical sector employed 64,000 people, in the electrical appliances and machinery sector, 53,000 people, and finally, in the automotive industry, 30,000 people.

Because of its proximity the United States has always held a high percentage of foreign investments. However, while the appearance of European investments in the beginning of the 1960s in the chemical industry, the machine industry, and the automotive industry caused a decrease in the share of American capital in these sectors, the percentage of US investments in the food industry showed a constant increase, from about 75 per cent in 1960 to 93.7 per cent in 1970. In 1970, the 6.3 per cent remaining originated, in order of importance, from Canada, Sweden, Switzerland and Venezuela. Since then, French (the case of BSN-Gervais Danone) and West German firms have also taken a foothold in Mexico.

The majority of US subsidiaries established in the Mexican food sector during the last twenty-five years were not simply the result of purchases or absorptions of existing Mexican firms. But starting in 1966, the number of these types of acquisitions by foreign firms has increased constantly: between 1966 and 1973, 75 per cent of the new foreign subsidiaries were the result of acquisitions. In government circles, it is estimated that such a denationalisation of the food industry was one of the major reasons for the 1973 Law on Foreign Investments which we have already described.

It is probable, although detailed statistics on this topic are lacking, that the percentage of the average holdings by foreigners in the food industry is larger than in other sectors. It appears that a much larger number of enterprises in this sector fall into the category of enterprises whose foreign participation is at least 75 per cent. Similarly, the number of foreign executives in this sector is higher than elsewhere.

Of the thirty-nine principal firms producing articles for human and animal food consumption, including non-alcoholic beverages, and whose name figures on the 'Fortune 500' list, thirty-two are established in Mexico. By comparison, of the same thirty-nine firms, thirty-one are located in Canada, twenty-three in France, twenty-two in Venezuela, and eighteen in Brazil. Taking aside the largest American firms in this sector and ranking the firms according to sales on the North American market alone, we notice that out of the top ten, seven are present in Mexico: Kraft Co., Esmark, Beatrice Foods, General Foods, Borden, Ralston Purina and Coca-Cola.

According to a recent study based on 1974 data, the foreign firms are particularly active in the production of food for babies and small children; 100 per cent of Mexico's supply comes from four foreign firms. One of them, Gerber Products, controls 85 per cent of the market. In the non-alcoholic beverages branch, foreign firms control more than 75 per cent of the market despite their small number: Coca-Cola, Pepsi-Cola and Seven Up. By itself, Coca-Cola holds 42 per cent of the market. In the intermediary food products branch, i.e. chemical products (colouring, additives, flavourings, extracts, and so forth) and receptacles, the Mexican market is totally under foreign control. As far as the milk products branch is concerned, as well as those products which are based on cereals, foreign holdings are also very large but less so than in the two branches mentioned above.

In 1975, eight large foreign firms[2] involved in milk products were established in Mexico: Carnation, Kraft Co., Nestlé, Wyeth International, Bristol Myers International, Read Johnson, the Pet Corp., and BSN-Gervais Danone; that is, six American firms, one Swiss firm, and one French firm. This list includes only the foreign firms whose principal production consists of milk products. The number of all foreign firms producing some milk products would be over thirty.

Looking at the sub-branches of the milk industry, we see that in some of these, foreign investments are sometimes very low or non-existent, while in others they form the majority. Thus for example, firms which pasteurise and distribute pasteurised milk, as well as those which produce ice cream, are all without exception completely controlled by Mexican capital. On the other hand, ten out of twelve firms in the condensed milk branch are under foreign control (with 96 per cent of invested capital, 98 per cent of the value added and 99 per cent of profits).

By receiving foreign industrial firms within its territory, the Mexican government has always aimed to contribute to an equilibrium in the balance of payments through the exports of these firms. It is obvious that in the food sector, the percentages of imports and exports in the gross value of production are lower than in other manufacturing industries; however, contrary to almost all other industries, exports in this sector are superior to imports because of the exporting activities of the foreign firms in this sector, limited as they may be.

In 1970, the export coefficient of the food industry firms under foreign control was 3.1 per cent and their import coefficient, 2.5 per cent; in both cases, import and export, these coefficients were higher than for Mexican food firms. Let us point out that this export coefficient of 3.1 per cent is comparable to that of the entire foreign manufacturing enterprises sector (which is 3 per cent), while the import coefficient is much smaller; 2.5 per cent as against 11.9 per cent. These figures indicate that in the food sector industries controlled by foreign capital, the vast majority of raw materials are of local origin and sales are almost totally destined for the local market. This is true even though the great majority of these firms are subsidiaries of multinationals based in the neighbouring country, the United States.

For food industry firms owned by United States interests, the return on invested capital was 9.1 per cent in 1972, which is less than the average for all US firms established in Mexico. But if we add to net profits the payments of royalties, of licensing fees and of technical assistance to the mother company, which constitute costs for the Mexican subsidiaries and a great deal of the profits for the mother companies, the rate of profitability of around 19.6 per cent in this sector is much higher than the average for all the other sectors, which is around 16.2 per cent.

Overview of food industry technology

The technological aspects of the food industry in Mexico have not yet been studied in depth, however, during the preparation of the First National Plan for Science and Technology, an expert group appointed by the government presented the following overview:

1 The Mexican food industry of a traditional, craft-like type does not have access to and does not create demand for new technological know-how.
2 The situation is practically the same for the small-sized food industry, where the introduction of new technologies for production, for conservation or for stocking is practically nil.
3 In medium-sized and large enterprises owned by Mexicans, technological progress is a little more noticeable; it is visible especially in their imports of machinery and industrial equipment and sometimes in the purchase of patented manufacturing processes; not a firm among these carries out its own technological research.
4 While large foreign firms apparently import a lot of technology from abroad, these are mostly purchases related to the use of registered trademarks. A representative sample of technology transfer contracts for the food industry presented in 1973 to the National Register for Technology Transfers, showed that 75 per cent of these contracts had clauses relative to the use of brand names and only 8 per cent to patented manufacturing processes.
5 During the last few years, foreign firms in the food sector have begun to invest locally in research and technology. However, these activities have had as their principal objective, if not their only objective, to create new products. In almost all these cases, it was more an adaptation of already existing products destined for the middle classes in urban locations.
6 Human resources available in Mexico for scientific and technological research in the food sector are very limited. The total number of people employed in research — transport, production, industrialisation, nutritional enrichment, and distribution — is not over 250 people, dispersed among a dozen small university research teams and another dozen or so public sector research units.

Notes

[1] Thomas Horst, *At Home Abroad: American Corporations in the Food Industry,* Cambridge, 1974.
[2] The US Company 'Borden' established itself in 1976.

4 The Danone Mexico Corporation

Introduction

Historical overview of the mother company: BSN-Gervais Danone

Before taking up the case study of Danone Mexico, let us briefly present the group BSN-Gervais Danone, the Mexican affiliate's mother company, and try to describe the main activities of this industrial conglomerate. Thus we will be better able to see where the developing country affiliates fit into the group's overall strategy.

In 1976, BSN-Gervais Danone was the result of a whole series of mergers, acquisitions and stock purchases — all of which had been accomplished in the relatively short period of ten years. If taken step-by-step, this history illustrates the multinationalisation of a firm which at the beginning did not really have international aspirations. This multinationalisation was the end-product of a strategy which can be described by two principles of action: to concentrate and increase market share on the one hand, and to diversify geographic location and product range on the other hand. To the casual observer two things stand out in the execution of this programme, even if the successful mergers and acquisitions might hide others which did not succeed: the apparently logical and at times even inevitable sequence of mergers and acquisitions, and the firm's rapid adaptation to change.

Originally we find the Souchon Company, a family-type firm created at the turn of the century and which produced glass packaging material, roughly 90 per cent bottles and 10 per cent packaging for perfume and pharmaceutical products. The firm at that time was part of a grouping of twelve firms controlled by different families and which pooled their technical and sales services. In 1964, all of these family-type enterprises merged into one highly-structured firm, the Souchon-Neuvesel Glass Makers.

The first concentration in the hollow-glass industry was actually the first step towards diversification. The conglomerate remained in the glass industry by merging in 1966 with Boussois Glass, which produced window glass for the housing market as well as windows and windscreens for the automobile market: this was a marriage between two glass firms, with Boussois contributing plants throughout Europe. In 1967 and 1968, the new firm, now named BSN (Boussois-Souchon-Neuvesel), continued its integration efforts within the glass industry and began to diversify into the manufacture of other glass containers and plastic packaging materials, finally buying into a firm in Barcelona, Spain.

In 1969-70, three factors led the Board of BSN to refine a European strategy in the flat glass sector and to give the firm a multi-European dimension. The first factor was a technological revolution, the discovery and the manufacturing of 'floated' glass,[1] which gradually began to substitute for traditionally-manufactured glass and windows. At the same time, the creation of the Common Market encouraged the breaking down of borders and brought European competition to France. But more than anything, the high cost of investments pointed to an inevitable regrouping between the large European manufacturers of flat glass. At this time there were five in Europe, only three in the United States and two in Japan. BSN's attempted merger with one of these, the French firm Saint-Gobain, having failed, the firm finally succeeded, between 1970 and 1972, in a new concentration and geographical diversification within the Common Market by grouping together a German glass manufacturing firm which it already controlled, and an important Belgian glass making group.

In the meantime, BSN was working towards a new strategy for its packaging line. In its search for new partners, the firm could rely on the experience it had acquired in 1920 when, as the Souchon company, it had become a shareholder in Evian and Badoit (water manufacturers and distributors), in order to ensure its market among bottle users. The decision was made to attempt to integrate both the contents and the packaging of the product. In 1970 negotiations succeeded with the purchase of Evian, which represented 30 per cent of the French mineral water market and 60 per cent of the market for baby foods. There then followed the acquisition of both the Kronenbourg and the European Brewery Co. (that is 45 per cent of the French beer market). At the same time, of course, the performance of the packaging branch began to improve.

The merger with Gervais Danone in 1973 represents the firm's last great diversification. Before 1973, the food industry branch of BSN had been very specifically limited to liquids and baby foods. It was small compared with the great international food companies. The merger with Gervais Danone opened up the market for solid foods, fresh or dried, in countries with a high standard of living and in developing countries, notably Brazil and Mexico, where Gervais Danone had just launched an operation.

These last ten years have thus marked an exceptional growth period for the firm. By 1976, the conglomerate included three well-structured sectors of activity: the food branch, which represented 54.7 per cent of annual turnover; the flat glass branch, with 29.3 per cent; and the packaging branch, with 16 per cent. Consolidated turnover, between 1966 and 1976, grew from 1 billion French francs to 11.7 billion French francs, and the number of employees increased from 15,000 to 61,600.

Such rapid results are of course due in great part to mergers and acquisitions rather than to internal growth, but they do reflect the dynamics of the firm's development.

With plants in most European countries — notably in Belgium, West Germany, Austria, Spain, United Kingdom, Switzerland, Netherlands, Italy — and

Table 4.1

List of Consolidated Firms
(As of 31 December 1977)

A. Firms Consolidated through Integration

Firm	Country	Percentages Control	Percentages Group's interest
Boussois Souchon Neuvesel			
Gervais Danone	France	Mother company	
Food Branch			
— EVIAN			
Couzan (Ste des Eaux Minerales de)	France	50.90	50.90
EBAMSA	Spain	49.00	49.00
L.H.D.E. (Laboratoire d'Hygiene Dermatologique d'Evian)	France	100.00	99.98
S.A.E.M.E. (S.A. des Eaux Minerales d'Evian)	France	100.00	100.00
Saint-Alban-les-Eaux (Ste des Eaux Minerales de)	France	49.37	49.37
Savoie-Plastique	France	100.00	100.00
S.E.V.P.F.E.	France	49.99	49.99
S.N.E.G.H.C.E. (ex-Casino Municipal d'Evian)	France	98.35	98.35
— KRONENBOURG			
Brasseries Kronenbourg	France	100.00	100.00
G.I.E. Tepral	France	100.00	100.00
Kronenbourg Italia	Italy	99.00	99.00
Kronenbourg Marketing	Switzerland	99.40	99.40
K.V.G. (Kronenbourg Vertriebs)	W. Germany	100.00	100.00
S.F.A.L. (Ste Financiere Alsacienne)	France	99.99	99.99
— SOCIETE EUROPEENNE DE BRASSERIES			
Alnot	France	74.40	74.40
Brasseries Dumesnil Freres et Cie	France	99.87	99.87
Diss	France	75.36	75.35
	France	98.67	98.54

Firm	Country	Percentages Control	Percentages Group's interest
Richter K.G.	W. Germany	73.88	72.56
— INTERNATIONAL FRESH PRODUCTS DEPARTMENT			
Godis (Continentale de Distribution)	Ivory Coast	99.64	99.64
Danone de Mexico (ex-Xalpa Industrial)	Mexico	49.00	49.00
Gerdabel Nederland	Netherlands	50.00	50.00
Gervais Danone Belgique	Belgium	99.98	99.96
Gervais Danone Italiana	Italy	100.00	100.00
Laticinios Poços de Caldas	Brazil	47.99	47.99
Sodiacam (Ste de Distribution Alimentaire au Cameroun)	The Cameroons	96.50	96.50
Packaging Branch			
— FRANCE			
Seprosy (Ste Europeenne pour la Transformation des Produits de Synthese)	France	99.99	99.99
— OTHER COUNTRIES			
Brasilver	Brazil	78.00	78.00
Nationaal Bezit	Netherlands	64.95	64.95
Sodispa	Spain	50.00	49.97
Sulver	Brazil	86.96	86.11
Vereenigde Glasfabrieken	Netherlands	99.89	64.88
Vidrieria Vilella	Spain	50.00	47.67
— VARIOUS FIRMS			
Durpoix et Fond	France	99.95	99.94

Company	Country		
S.C.E.B. (Ste Commerciale Europeenne de Brasseries)	France	100.00	100.00
S.E.B. (Ste Europeenne de Brasseries)	France	100.00	100.00
Sobcal (ex-Agenaise de Boissons)	France	99.92	99.92
Sobest	France	100.00	100.00
Soblor (ex-Messire)	France	99.95	99.95
Sobonor (ex-Brasserie de Laval)	France	100.00	100.00
Socodem	France	66.54	61.80
U.F.B. (Union Financiere de la Brasserie)	France	100.00	100.00
— DIEPAL			
Diepal	France	100.00	100.00
— GALLIA			
Gallia (Ste Dietetique)	France	99.98	99.98
— PANZANI MILLIAT FRERES			
Coper	France	99.77	99.76
Ferico	France	49.95	49.95
L'Industrie Alimentaire	Dahomey	92.02	92.02
Milliat Freres Cameroun	The Cameroons	65.80	65.80
Panzani Milliat Freres S.A.	France	99.99	99.99
Riccardi	Italy	100.00	99.99
Semoulerie de Bellevue	France	99.97	99.96
Societe Fonciere et Commerciale du Silo de la Madrague	France	99.66	99.62
— DEPARTEMENT INTERNATIONAL PRODUITS SECS			
Hijos de Francisco Saula	Spain	49.00	49.00
Milliat Saula	Spain	49.00	49.00
— GERVAIS DANONE FRANCE			
Gervais Danone France	France	100.00	100.00
Laiterie des Moulineaux	France	99.97	99.97
Laiterie de Villecomtal	France	50.21	50.21
Martin	France	98.75	98.75
— STENVAL			
Stenval S.A.	France	99.99	99.99
Stenval Belgique	Belgium	99.98	99.96
— GERVAIS DANONE ALLEMAGNE			
Danone GmbH	W. Germany	100.00	100.00
Gervais Danone A.G.	W. Germany	98.21	98.21
Gervais Danone GmbH	Austria	100.00	98.21

Company	Country		
A.I.V. (Applications Industrielles du Verre)	France	99.80	65.96
Barrel	France	69.07	34.50
Boussois S.A.	France	100.00	66.09
Daguillon	France	49.33	32.61
Daver	France	95.81	63.33
Glaces et Verres	France	87.17	57.61
Glacisol	France	99.95	66.06
Glaverouest	France	99.94	66.05
Miroiteries de l'Est	France	75.58	49.95
Normanver	France	99.96	66.06
Omnium de Miroiteries	France	99.93	66.05
Personnaz	France	99.56	65.80
Picon	France	65.95	43.59
Ponsinet	France	94.94	62.75
Prover	France	99.40	65.70
S.G.M. Eurover	France	90.63	59.90
Siglaver	France	99.95	66.06
Soframir (Ste Française d'Application de Miroiterie	France	99.70	65.89
Sovico	France	99.86	66.00
Sovig	France	99.84	65.99
Sovilor	France	99.88	66.01
Vitrage Isolar	France	89.00	58.76
— BENELUX — ITALY			
De Maas (Machinale Glasfabrik)	Netherlands	100.00	66.09
Glaverbel S.A.	Belgium	100.00	66.09
Mirodan	Belgium	65.00	42.77
Miroiteries de Charleroi S.A. (Mirox)	Belgium	99.99	66.09
Mirvitral	Belgium	99.98	66.08
Multipane	Belgium	99.82	65.82
Sovitec S.A.	Belgium	99.97	66.08
Splintex Belge	Belgium	99.70	65.89
Thermopane Suisse	Switzerland	51.00	33.71
Verreries Gobbe Hocquemiller	Belgium	99.55	65.80
Vetritalia	Italy	100.00	66.09
Vetrocom	Italy	100.00	66.09
— GERMANY — AUSTRIA			
Bauglas Grosshandel	Austria	100.00	36.66

Firm	Country	Percentages Control	Group's interest
Bauglas Industrie	Germany	99.32	36.41
Eomag (Erste Osterreichische Machinglas Industrie A.G.)	Austria	100.00	36.66
Eugen Frederich	Germany	100.00	36.66
Flachglas A.G. Delog-Deta	Germany	72.92	36.66
G.F. Schweikert	Germany	55.60	20.39
Glaszentrum Ruhr et Cie	Germany	100.00	36.66
Glaszentrum Stoermer	Germany	100.00	36.66
Moosbrunner Glasfabrik GmbH	Austria	100.00	36.66
Spiegel Union Flabeg	Germany	100.00	36.66
— OTHER FIRMS			
B.F.G. Glassgroup (Groupement d'interet economique G.V.B., Boussois S.A. Flachglas)	France	100.00	56.28
Celo	Spain	42.98	28.41
Dahlbusch Verwaltungs A.G.	Germany	81.98	47.00
Mecaniver	Belgium	66.11	66.09
Providro	Brazil	41.00	24.52
Expanver	France	99.99	99.99
— VARIOUS FIRMS			
Argiles de Saint-Loup (Ste Nouvelle des)	France	99.95	99.95
Cofive (Cie Financiere et Verriere)	Belgium	99.82	99.82
Compagnie Gervais Danone	France	100.00	100.00
Finaver	France	99.97	99.97
Gerdabel France	France	50.00	50.00
Ingetec	France	96.00	94.30
Lyon Air	France	77.60	77.60
Sadiep	France	99.77	99.77
Sepiver	France	100.00	99.95
Verzola	France	99.98	99.98

B. Firms Consolidated through Equivalence

Firm	Country	Percentages Control	Group's interest
Food branch			
— EVIAN			
S.I.A.O. (Ste des Industries Agricoles et Alimentaires de l'Ouest)	France	10.88	34.99
Sicapom	France	—	29.74
— KRONENBOURG			
Felske	France	33.90	33.90
S.C.B.K. (Ste Congolaise des Brasseries Kronenbourg)	Congo	37.48	37.48
— SOCIETE EUROPEENNE DE BRASSERIES			
Sobrhone	France	49.78	49.78
— DIEPAL			
Difal	France	49.80	49.80
— DEPARTEMENT INTERNATIONAL PRODUITS SECS			
Prodial	Spain	50.00	50.00
— DEPARTEMENT INTERNATIONAL PRODUITS FRAIS			
Dansul	Brazil	—	23.95
Leite Sol	Brazil	47.99	47.99
Packaging Branch			
— FRANCE			
Strafrance	France	48.96	48.95
Flat Glass Branch			
— OTHER FIRMS			
Financiera Alavesa	Spain	20.03	13.24
Vidrierias de Llodio	Spain	—	13.24
Various Firms			
Sogevals	France	41.88	41.88

in Latin America (Mexico, Brazil and Argentina) as well as in Africa, where it controls trading companies in the Ivory Coast, the Cameroons and Dahomey — BSN-Gervais Danone has in fact become multinational within a few years. On the preceding three pages, listings taken from the 1977 annual report show the names of the consolidated firms of the group, their location by country, and the percentage of direct or indirect holdings by the mother company, with a breakdown by sectors of activity. The long term objectives that the Board of Directors set for themselves for the decade to come and that the group's President made public during the ordinary shareholders' assembly of 1976, are aimed at developing the multinational character of the firm and notably its activities in the food industry sector. This background should be kept in mind in order to appreciate the analysis of Danone Mexico's activities.

Activities of BSN-Gervais Danone in developing countries

The group's first industrial involvement in developing countries dates back to 1963, the year when the Boussois Co. (by way of the successive mergers described above, this firm became part of BSN-Gervais Danone) bought a minority share in the ·Brazilian firm Providro, which in its factory in Caçapava produced flat glass for the automobile industry. By the end of 1976, Providro was employing more than 700 people, of which only five were foreign staff sent from Paris.

In 1970 three years before its merger with BSN, Gervais Danone had made a deal with a Brazilian firm in the milk products sector, Sociedade Laticinios Poços de Caldas, a franchising deal later reinforced by successive stock purchases. By the end of 1976, BSN-Gervais Danone controlled 48 per cent of the capital. There also the number of employees from the Parisian home office had been considerably reduced over the years. By the end of 1976, there were only three French staff: the Director of Studies and Research, a technical junior executive, and an executive in the marketing department, all three depending hierarchically on a Brazilian superior. The five factories which the firm operated produced yogurt, desserts, fresh cheese and milk for consumption. The firm had nearly 2,000 employees by the end of 1976.

BSN-Gervais Danone was also established in Venezuela, where it has a 16 per cent minority share in the Templex Co., a producer of flat glass.

In Latin America, the group's latest industrial investment was the one in Mexico which we are studying here.

Let us add that in Argentina the group had taken a minority share, but without any management responsibility, in the Vasa SA Company, also involved in flat glass production. This share was sold in 1975.

In Africa, the French group controls companies in the Cameroons in the Ivory Coast and in Dahomey. These are trading companies which sell mostly imported products.

Table 4.2

BSN-Gervais Danone in 1976

Turnover, profits and employees

	Consolidated T/O less internal sales (millions of F. francs)	Net profits (millions of F. francs)	No. of employees
France	6,883	70	33,077
Industrialised countries less France (West Germany, Spain, Belgium, Austria, Netherlands.)	4,171	—30	25,608
Sub-total	11,054	40	58,685
Developing countries			
Mexico	23	—4	135
Brazil	349	8	2,628
Argentina	2	—	—
Africa	178	2	159
Sub-total	552	6	2,922
Total	11,606	16	61,607
% ind. countries	95.25%	86.96%	95.26%
% devel. countries	4.75%	43.04%	4.74%

Table 4.2 gives a good idea of the overall activities of affiliates and other firms related to BSN-Gervais Danone in developing countries during the year 1976.[2] The turnover was 552 million French francs and represented 4.75 per cent of the group's total turnover, the other 95.25 per cent having been generated in Europe. The share of net profits from developing countries was 13 per cent; it was relatively large for that year but is not necessarily significant. In fact 1976 was a very bad year for the group's firms located in industrialised countries (except for France), which together lost 30 million French francs and thus artificially increased, if we may say so, the percentage of the profits originating from developing countries compared with profits from other markets.

As to the number of employees in firms located in developing countries, it amounted to 4.7 per cent of the group's total and numbered nearly 3000 persons. In conclusion, one could say that if the developing countries represent, for the mother company, a considerable potential market and will probably play an active part in the process of multinationalisation aimed for by the Board of Directors, their role is still very limited within the group's overall activities.

The activities of Danone Mexico

The main stages of development of Danone Mexico — Autumn 1972 to December 1976

The following pages are a summary of the dates and facts which marked Danone Mexico's main stages of development. The need for such a description is not so much to be sought in the exceptional or exemplary nature of the firm's history, which is still very short, but rather in the exposition of the precise steps which were followed by a multinational firm which wanted to establish itself in Mexico.

Autumn 1972

In 1972, Gervais Danone was fully expanded and its executives, noticing the excellent results obtained in Brazil where sales of yogurt had more than doubled in one year, thought that a new implantation in another Latin American country would have the same success provided that it was well managed. They thought that Mexico, with a population of more than 50 million inhabitants and one of the highest levels of development in that part of the world, was a potential market of the first order. The decision was thus taken in Paris to look for a Mexican partner wishing to associate with the firm to produce and sell yogurts and milk-based desserts. The necessity to be able to count on a regular supply of raw materials, i.e. high-quality fresh milk, would guide the choice of the local partner.

Following several trips to Mexico, the choice was made to take on a Mexican industrialist who was already active in the production of fruit juices and especially in the sale of pasteurised milk. The future associate had some land, a plant for milk pasteurisation, a certain experience in the collecting of fresh milk from farmers, and a distribution system for his beverage production. Moreover, he had just created, in September 1972, the company Xalpa Industrial SA, with a capital of 500,000 pesos ($40,000), which could constitute the adequate legal structure for a joint venture.

January 1973

A series of interviews led Gervais Danone to evolve concrete partnership plans within the framework of Xalpa Industrial. A *letter of intention* written in January, 1973 made clear the principal terms:

> Gervais Danone will bring its brand and its techniques and will send its technicians to train on-the-job Xalpa Industrial's technicians. The Mexican firm will pay for travel and per diem expenses, but Gervais Danone will pay its technicians' salaries.
>
> Gervais Danone will also contribute 980,000 pesos (finally 1,125,000) in fresh capital and will take it upon itself to look for a bank loan for the neces-

37

sary financing to purchase machinery, equipment, and for operating capital during the start-up period. It is estimated that a loan of 3,500,000 pesos would be sufficient at that stage.

From his side the Mexican partner will contribute the legal structure which exists in the form of Xalpa Industrial, created the previous year, some physical installations and the assurance of a regular supply of fresh milk.

May 1973

The operation described in the letter of intent came to fruition with an increase in Xalpa Industrial's capital from 500,000 to 2,500,000 pesos. Gervais Danone held 49 per cent of the shares and the Mexican partner 51 per cent. In addition, the positions of president and general manager were to be held by the Mexican group.

October 1973 New increase in the capital of Xalpa Industrial

The specialists sent by Gervais Danone to start up the operation noticed that existing installations were inadequate and that the local leadership did not have sufficient experience to succeed in such a venture. It was decided to increase the capital once again, from 2,500,000 to 4,500,000 pesos, in order to finance the purchase of necessary production equipment. The Mexican associate subscribed his part and the percentage participation of Gervais Danone thus remained unchanged. A new Mexican general manager was appointed.

November 1973

The legal finalisation of the merger between BSN and Gervais Danone having occurred in 1973, the new group BSN-Gervais Danone ratified the accord concluded by Gervais Danone in Mexico.

December 1973

BSN-Gervais Danone and its Mexican associate agreed on stipulations concerning conditions regulating the right to reciprocal preemption of Xalpa Industrial's shares.

March 1974

The first Danone products were put on the market: natural and fruit yogurts, custard and puddings. The start-up phase was slow. The turnover in 1974 was 9,401,000 pesos and the financial year's exercise ended up with a loss of 8,000,000 pesos. Experts from BSN-Gervais Danone returned from a study mission in the field and recommended a complete reorganisation of production and distribution. New financial resources would have to be injected to sustain the long term development of the firm.

October 1974

The French partner committed itself to giving the firm the financial means to ensure its development. Reciprocally, the Mexican partner, still in the majority, accepted to hand over management to the French group. Thus, starting in June 1975, a Frenchman trained in the mother company and specialised in mass consumption fresh products, became general manager.

November and December 1975

1975 was still a difficult year for the firm. Despite an important increase in production and turnover, the financial year ended with a loss of more than 12,000,000 pesos. To avoid closing down the operation, more capital was needed. The Mexican partner did not provide his part and BSN-Gervais Danone thus took over effective control of the firm. The capital was now 20,000,000 pesos. BSN-Gervais Danone subscribed the entire increase, that is, 15.5 million pesos, and thus held 88.5 per cent of the shares, with the Mexican partner reduced to 11.5 per cent of the shares.

But the new Law of 1973 (which we described in chapter 2) did not allow a foreign investor to hold majority control in a Mexican firm. The only recourse was to the 'fidéicommis' foreseen by the Mexican law: BSN-Gervais Danone remained a 49 per cent shareholder, and 39.5 per cent of the shares were deposited in 'fidéicommis' in a Mexican bank, which at the end of three years (a time period which could be prolonged) would have to offer these shares for sale. However, only Mexicans or Mexican firms would be allowed to buy these shares.

December 1976

Xalpa Industrial SA, officially changed its name and became Danone Mexico SA. During 1976, two de facto devaluations of the peso had a considerable effect on the results of the financial exercise. At the end of August, the government decided to abandon the fixed rate of exchange of the peso with respect to the US dollar. This rate, which had been 12.5 pesos per dollar since 1954, began to float around 20 until November, when it went down to 28. The peso steadied during the following months and since then it has remained at around 22 to 23 pesos to the dollar.

The 1976 financial exercise ended up with a loss of almost 21,000,000 pesos, of which 16,000,000 were imputable to exchange rate losses caused by the firm's large debt in hard currencies. Thus, in March 1977, there was need again to increase the capital, which was brought to 55,000,000 pesos, and this was followed by yet another influx of capital to finance the firm's investment programme.

Advantages obtained by plant construction

We have already described the conditions for foreign plant installations in Mexico and the restrictions provided by the Law on Foreign Investments. This investment code did not provide for any tariff or fiscal exemptions for either foreign or national firms wishing to establish themselves in Mexico, contrary to the postwar period when the government was actively promoting industrialisation. Danone Mexico was no exception to the rule.

Nevertheless, as any other Mexican firm in the same conditions, Danone Mexico could benefit from the Law of 9 July 1972 for the promotion of regionalisation, by virtue of its geographical location. This Law was based on the need to orient investments towards the less-industrialised regions of the country, in order to reduce differences in living standards between urban and rural regions. Moreover, the Law favoured small and medium-sized enterprises whose raw materials would come from fishing, agriculture and livestock breeding activities.

This Law divided the Mexican territory into three zones according to their degree of industrial concentration. The Danone Mexico factory, located about 60 km. from Mexico City in Huehuetoca, was in the zone most favoured by this Law. The advantages, granted for a period of five years, were both tariff-oriented and fiscal. Thus, Danone Mexico obtained an exemption of up to 70 per cent of customs duties on imports of industrial machinery, and its rate for federal income tax on sales (Ingresos Mercantiles) was 2.5 per cent instead of 4 per cent. In addition, the firm had the opportunity to depreciate more quickly its assets related to industrial machinery, which in effect also decreased the tax on profits.

Production

(a) Environment

The Danone Mexico factory in Huehuetoca is located in an essentially agricultural region which offers few jobs to the 16,000 inhabitants of the 'county' (which groups together several villages). Besides Danone Mexico, three other industries were established in the 'county': a ready-to-wear factory with 300 employees, the majority being women; a sheet-plate industry employing 120 people; and a small Swedish firm manufacturing explosives and employing 20 people.

The socio-economic environment was characterised by a very high unemployment rate and a living standard closer to that of the countryside than to city standards despite the proximity of the capital. Seven primary schools existed for children between 6 to 12, and for a few years already there had also been a secondary school. For the population, however, the arrival of Danone Mexico in the area represented above anything else a new source of employment. The firm was thus very welcome from the start.

The choice of site was not dictated by geographical, social or fiscal considerations. Danone's Mexican partner owned a large property in Huehuetoca on which he had installed (near his farm with 300 milk cows) the industrial machinery necessary for a small pasteurisation unit and for bottling fresh milk. One of the clauses of the partnership had stipulated that the Mexican partner would provide land and some existing facilities in addition to a legal corporate structure.

(b)   Range of products

In 1976, the range of products was still very limited (see Table 4.3). It consisted basically yogurts, both natural and with fruits (strawberries, pineapples, lemons, mangos, peaches and blackberries) sold under the brand name Danone and of water-based gelatines sold under the brand name Dany. In 1974, the company was also manufacturing puddings and custards; their production ceased in 1975, the very high level of demand for yogurt having absorbed the plant's entire production capacity.

Under the brand name Xalpa, Danone Mexico also sells orange juice and flavoured milks, which the Mexican partner was already producing before his association with the French group. The small volume of this production did not require complicated industrial machinery; the production was actually effected by a subcontractor who rented out his own installations for a few hours a week. In fact, the share of these items in the firm's overall production and turnover was very unimportant, as shown in Table 4.4 which summarises Danone Mexico's financial data for the years 1974-77. It seems that these two products, inherited from the 1973 partnership, were somewhat neglected. Sold under the brand name Xalpa without any advertising, these drinks had a very low-profile brand name compared with a concentrated and dynamic competition. In addition,

Table 4.3

Danone Mexico — Range of Products

	1974	1975	1976	1977
Yogurts	natural	natural	natural	natural
	with fruits	with fruits	with fruits	with fruits
Desserts	custard	custard	water-based	water and
	milk-based	milk-based	gelatine	milk-based
	gelatine	gelatine		gelatines
	pudding	pudding		
		water-based		
		gelatine		
Beverages	pure fruit juice	pure fruit juice	pure fruit juice	pure fruit juice
	fruit-based	fruit-based	fruit-based	fruit-based
	beverage	beverage	beverage	beverage
	flavoured milk	flavoured milk	flavoured milk	

they were not distributed by the sales department of Danone Mexico, a department which benefited from much of the management's attention.

Such a limited range of products — yogurt representing 75 per cent of total turnover — is without a doubt one of the present weaknesses of the firm. By the end of 1976, Danone's four competitors all had a more varied range of products.

The firm is conscious of the danger: its medium term development plans provide for the addition of new flavours to its existing range of yogurts as well for the development of new products.

(c) Production and capacity

The firm's dynamism was reflected in the frequency of successive increases in industrial capacity in the Huehuetoca plant. From its inception in the beginning of 1974, the plant's capacity grew from 6 tons per day to 24 tons per day in 1977 with intermediate steps of 10 and 14 tons per day. The factory itself, conceived as a central nucleus to which could be added modules for expansion, is actually in its second stage of growth. Recently, the firm acquired a new tract of land for its future installations, thus demonstrating its intention to reinvest in the same location for a longer term development.

As far as production is concerned, Table 4.4 shows the progression of production by year and item. Let us simply say here that the increase in production of yogurts and desserts was fairly large: it went from 36 tons in 1974 for yogurt to 2,420 tons in 1976; for desserts, it went from 36 tons in 1974 to 802 in 1976. The 1977 estimates were over-optimistic but the pattern of growth was maintained, that is, about 25 per cent for yogurts and over 70 per cent for desserts. On the other hand, production of beverages, which had doubled between 1974 and 1975, stabilised in 1976 and actually decreased in 1977.

Table 4.4
Danone-Mexico — Production and Turnover

	1974	1975	1976	1977 (estimates as of 31 March, 1976)
Yogurts (tons)	163	990	2,420	2,910
Desserts (tons)	36	133	802	1,307
Beverages (hectolitres)	12,138	31,800	36,605	7,720
Turnover (Thousands of pesos)	9,401	27,531	68,575	94,025
Net results: (losses) (Thousands of pesos)	(7,980)	(12,557)	(21,710)[1]	(2,650)[2]

[1]Of which 16,040 exchange rate losses (devaluation of the peso in August and September 1976).
[2]Excluding 7,000,000 in exchange rate losses, the operational profit was 4,300,000 pesos.

(d)   Raw materials

Raw materials used in the production of yogurt are fresh milk, skimmed powdered milk, fermentation components, and fruits to mix with yogurt. For juices
and flavoured beverages, the raw materials are sugar, colouring agents, flavour-
ing agents, oranges, grapefruits, fruit concentrates and chemical preservatives.
For the milk-based or water-based gelatines one must use colouring agents,
sugar and gelatinising catalysts (cornflour and extracts of algae).

Table 4.5

Summary Table

Raw Materials
(thousands of pesos)

	1975	1976
Raw Materials		
Local	9,648	26,683
Imported	1,752	5,441
Total	11,400	32,124
% Imported	15.3%	16.9%

Note: Exchange rates: 1975: 100 pesos = $8.00
1976: 2/3 of amounts: 100 pesos = $8.00
1/3 of amounts: 100 pesos = $4.54

Table 4.5, the summary table, which indicates raw material purchases, also
includes packaging materials and labels as well as cartons for shipment.

The percentage of purchases of imported raw materials, which have a negative
effect on balance of payments, is very small: 15.3 per cent in 1975 and 16.9 per
cent in 1976. This category consists mostly of skimmed powdered milk (60 per
cent of imported raw materials in 1975 and 61 per cent in 1976) which must be
imported because of a certain insufficiency in the local supply of fresh milk.

Regular supplies of fresh milk constitute the major problem facing the plant's
management. In fact, since the beginning of 1977, demand for fresh milk has
been around 11,000 litres per day, and given the scarcity of fresh milk (especially
during the dry period between October and March), competition between pas-
teurising enterprises is very keen. The floor price of milk is fixed each year by the
government and varies according to geographical zones. In March 1977, it was
3.8 pesos per litre in the region of Huehuetoca, but the factory paid 4.6 pesos per
litre. The firm's products are not price-controlled by the government. Thus, for

certain milk products, such as condensed milk and powdered milk, the firm's purchasing policy can be relatively flexible.

Danone Mexico does not buy directly from the producers as do certain other foreign firms such as Nestlé. It relies on daily deliveries by an intermediary firm which belongs to its Mexican partner. (We noted in the history of BSN-Gervais Danone's implantation in Mexico, that the Mexican partner had to be able to provide or at least guarantee a supply of fresh milk.) In fact, the very irregular supply and its erratic quality and quantity made the organisation of production very difficult and, from our point of view, the firm's growth potential has been seriously affected by this fact. Systematic recourse to imports of skimmed powdered milk, whose price is lower than fresh milk anyway, could resolve the problem. But this solution is forbidden by the government, which controls these imports very strictly in order to protect national milk production and also in order to force the large firms operating in the milk products industry to develop by themselves new milk-producing districts. Requests for imports which, in principle, should not go over 10 per cent of total needs, have to be renewed every three months by a State organisation called the Conasupo, which has total control over foreign purchases of certain foodstuffs. This requires extensive bureaucratic paperwork and leads to very tight bargaining situations.

In order to be efficient, such a policy would have to be accompanied by adequate customs controls: in fact, the black market in skimmed powdered milk and related smuggling activities are flourishing and highly profitable.

Distribution

For reasons of the commercial policy of the company, we are not authorised to reveal here the number of salesmen or of sales inspectors, or the distribution of sales centres amond the small traditional shops, the supermarkets, and the State stores where some very poor people or certain categories of civil servants have the right to shop at substantial discounts. We regret this because the exact numbers which we could obtain in the field might have given a good idea, by extrapolation, of the socio-economic strata of Danone products' buyers.

But we can describe briefly the work of salesmen in Mexico City. In the interior, sales are through wholesalers and the system is not typical of Danone Mexico. In Mexico City, distribution is performed directly by the salesmen without going through wholesalers. Each salesman is responsible for one or several sales routes which he covers two or three times a week in his van. The salesman does not deliver previously ordered merchandise; he goes to the small grocery stores and supermarkets on his route and in each case after looking at what has been sold since his last visit, he suggests to the manager-owner of the grocery store or to the manager of the fresh milk products section of the supermarket, what is required to renew his stock. He does not content himself merely with selling merchandise; he is the one who actually sets up the yogurt trays in the section reserved for Danone products. In the supermarkets, Danone yogurts are next to those of the competition. In the traditional stores, where weekly sales are sometimes less than thirty 125-gram pots, it often happens that only one brand name is represented. The salesman is also responsible for the 'sell by date' which is printed on his products and, at each delivery, he must replace the pots which are past the deadline. (Let us note in passing that merchandise in this category represented 2 per cent of the 1976 production).

Economic performance

(a) Sales, turnover, and results

Table 4.2, which illustrated the progression of production, sales and net results since the firm's creation, calls for a few comments. Sales of yogurts have more than doubled each year and it seems that since 1976 they have progressed at a constant rate. The growth in sales of desserts was assured by the water-based gelatine which was put on the market during the last quarter of 1975. Sales of flavoured milk and juices stabilised after a rapid period of growth in 1975. And in 1977, after flavoured milks were abandoned because of their low profitability and also because of the low milk supply which we have already mentioned, sales of beverages dropped below the level reached in 1974.

Because of the absence of price controls on these products, turnover followed this large expansion in sales and went from 9.5 million pesos in 1974 to over 68 million in 1976. A good rate of increase was maintained in 1977: sales topped 90 million pesos. The share of yogurt sales in this turnover is by far the most important.

The net result for the first four years of activity is negative. Losses increased from nearly 8 million pesos in 1974 to 20.6 million in 1976, of which more than 16 million can be attributed to exchange rate losses due to the two de facto devaluations of the peso in August and November 1976. These losses had to be offset by successive increases in the firm's capital. As for 1977, the situation shows a marked improvement: losses only amounted to 3.2 million pesos and if one takes into account a loss of 7 million pesos due to drops in the exchange rate, then the operation itself showed a profit.

The firm's managers attribute the bad 1974 and 1975 performances (years when there were no losses due to changes in rates of exchange) to an inadequate distribution system, a bad presentation of products and a lack of rigorous management.

(b) Financial policy

The financial policy of affiliates and subsidiaries of multinationals is often the subject of analysis by economists, who attribute to the financial behaviour of these firms the responsibility for the balance of payments deficits which are more and more noticeable in the developing countries where these firms are installed. Often these economists notice that subsidiaries do not draw on the local financial market, thus diverting some potentially important transactions which could help develop that market.

It is interesting to analyse in a little more depth the situation of BSN-Gervais Danone's subsidiary in Mexico, even if the small scale of the enterprise makes generalisation difficult. Only by putting this question into the more general context of Mexico's financial market structure can one attempt some clarification.

Mexico's policy of industrialisation through an import substitution strategy, encouraged by the government in the postwar period, did not bring with it the expected remedy to an increasing instability in the balance of payments. In order to produce in Mexico, it was necessary to import more and more machines, intermediary goods, capital and technology. In fact, imports were always in excess of exports, and currency brought in by tourism and certain services (which, from 1960 to 1963, still made up for 35 per cent of the deficit in the balance of trade) has played a progressively lesser part over the last ten years. In order to re-establish some equilibrium, the private sector as well as the public sector had massive recourse to foreign loans and especially to the Euro-Currency market. We observed earlier the consequences of this situation in some detail. Let us note here that since 1973, the local money market has been extremely tight and it is very, very difficult for a medium sized enterprise to get a loan in pesos. To overcome this difficulty and get the economy moving again, one of the first measures of financial policy taken up by the new government, which came into power in December 1976, was to diminish the required deposits of banks and, thus, to open up more possibilities for credit in pesos. This measure, which came somewhat late in any event, faced a new difficulty: the rate of inflation, which had been maintained below 10 per cent until 1975 (quite a performance in Latin America), would top 20 per cent in the following year.

Under these circumstances Danone Mexico, along with many other firms, both foreign and national, had to resort to different types of loans in local and foreign currencies. Danone did not have another choice, especially since the Mexican government has asked Mexican banks not to extend loans to foreign multinationals or their subsidiaries established in the country. This measure was to maintain credit possibilities for national firms.

Let us note in passing that the rate of interest on loans obtained from foreign banks has always been lower than the rate offered by national or local banks. And of course the interest rate on the loan made by Danone Mexico directly from its mother company was much lower than the rates usually established in Mexico. Let us also note that in order to protect national banking activities and raise obstacles for 'fictitious' loans, fiscal legislation heavily taxes interests paid to foreign banks: 26.7 per cent if the lending bank has an official representative in Mexico, and 47.75 per cent if it has none.

Besides these fiscal measures, and bearing in mind the scarcity of capital on the local market, it is generally true that a subsidiary or a multinational firm have much less difficulty than a national firm (which could be a competitor) in obtaining loans from a foreign bank, especially if it is a medium sized enterprise. In fact, contrary to a national firm with no branches outside of the country, the multinational has at its disposal, in its country of origin, a whole network of banking relations. In addition, if worse comes to worse, it can always request a loan from its mother company; this process may not be automatic, but if such a request is well-documented and integrates itself into the development plans of the firm, the mother company will seldom turn it down.

In this particular case, the foreign firms or joint ventures competing with Danone Mexico were all in the same basic situations, and thus the notion of competition keeps its true sense (with the exception of one 100 per cent Mexican firm, which was also a competitor).

Employment

(a) Personnel structure

Employment in Danone Mexico has increased constantly since the firm's creation. From 70 employees in 1974, the work force grew to 170 people in 1977. These 170 jobs represent very little in comparison with the 228,000 jobs offered in 1975 by the 8,350 food industry firms which employ more than five people. We have seen, however, that at the regional level, the jobs offered in the Huehuetoca plant played an important role in the local employment market.

Foreign staff was always very small in numbers and decreased in time. In 1975 and 1976, there were still four foreign employees: the general manager, the sales director, and two high-level technicians who worked in the plant. By the end of 1976, two Mexicans had taken over the jobs filled by two of the French expatriates. In 1977, the only foreigners left were the general manager and one technician who was acting as the plant's manager.

(b) Salaries

Gross salaries amounted to 5.3 million pesos in 1975, 10.1 million in 1976 (14.9 per cent of turnover), and close to 30 million in 1977 (16.6 per cent of turnover).

The firm's wage policy has been fairly simple. The firm is independent from the mother company in this respect, but the establishment of the firm in Mexico is too recent for the firm to have formulated a specific salary and social policy. For the moment, Danone Mexico is sticking close to legal norms practised in Mexico. Thus, in January 1977, the lowest salaries were at least equal to the minimum legal salary determined and annually readjusted by the government. At that date, of the 126 people employed by the firm only 28 were receiving the minimum salary. In all the cases, they were workers in the Huehuetoca plant whose jobs did not require previous professional training.

The base salary of salesmen and distributors was augmented, through commissions on sales, by a sum which represented on the average two-thirds of their base salary, or in total more than 1.5 times the legal minimum. To determine the salary level of specialised workers, employees, and junior and higher level executives, the firm's directors first took into account the practices of competing firms in the same branch. But unlike salary levels maintained by large foreign firms established in the country, those of Danone Mexico were generally lower.

If one considers the scale of salaries in the firm, one notices that Danone Mexico is no exception to the general rule according to which, in developing countries, the difference between the lowest salary and the highest salary is much greater than in industrialised countries.

(c) Social policy

Social policy is dictated in the first place by legislation which requires every firm to register its personnel with social security.

As in the majority of Mexican firms, executives and administrative staff who are called in Mexico 'confidence' personnel are not unionised. Other employees are automatically integrated into the firm's union as soon as they are hired. This union is affiliated to a milk workers' union which groups together the 'workers and employees in the milk products industry'. Every two years, this union renegotiates the collective contract and the internal regulations which fix salaries and follow the principal clauses of Mexico's social legislation.

This firm has not had a strike or a serious labour conflict since its creation. The work week is 48 hours, and the workers in the Huehuetoca plant work in shifts. The night shift, however, only works 42 hours per week.

Internal regulations of the plant provide for a 100 per cent indemnity for overtime of less than nine hours per week, and 200 per cent beyond that. In practice, for the year 1976, these indemnities did not amount to much: overtime for all the personnel represented only 0.87 per cent of gross salaries.

The few rare social items not foreseen by the Law but applied by the firm concern holidays and vacations: the collective contract adds four days. Likewise, all personnel are allowed to buy, at wholesale prices, 30 yogurts and 60 gelatine desserts per week. In addition, during the break for the principal meal, the workers can consume yo urts and desserts if they choose.

On the other hand, the firm has not yet done anything about housing, pensions or sports activities (which is common practice in Mexico). One must remember, however, that Danone Mexico has only been established there since 1974 and that management is still bound by other priorities. The absence of a canteen in the plant might seem surprising for a factory in the food industry, even taking into account difficulties caused by differences in production cycles and work shifts, and the different schedules required for preparation, conditioning and storage of products. The workers do have a place where they can eat meals that they have brought themselves, but there is no company restaurant where subsidised hot meals are served. Such a canteen would be useful given that

·workers only have a half-hour for their meal and thus it is not possible for them to get home.

The strict application of the two fundamental clauses of social legislation, minimum salary and registration with social security, is implicit. However, it is interesting to note that in Mexico, about 40 per cent of the active population is not covered by these benefits which often represent, for the low-salaried classes, some security, professional satisfaction and the hope of a better life.

Along this line, a well-known fact is that foreign firms and those involved in joint ventures generally do more in these two areas than the small and medium sized local firms. The mother companies of multinationals, having become more and more conscious of the good image that they must maintain or acquire in developing countries, would not even attempt to ignore the elementary requirements of social legislation. The local directors of Danone Mexico estimate that improvements must still be made in the social and salary benefits actually being offered in order to match standards in the group's subsidiaries established in industrialised countries. They are seriously thinking about setting up an action programme in this area as soon as the firm's financial results show an improvement.

(d)   Productivity

It is already very difficult to compare productivity of plants producing the same product when they are located in the same country or at the very least in a group of countries with comparable economic conditions; it is an almost impossible task when one of those plants is in an industrialised country and the other in a developing country.

As an illustration it is interesting to compare a few data of the Huehuetoca plant with those of a BSN-Gervais Danone plant located in Rotselaar, Belgium, whose products are about the same. The industrial machinery is no more or less sophisticated than that of the Mexican plant; the only difference is in the cleaning of machines, which in Belgium is done in a closed circuit.

In 1976, the Rotselaar plant produced a little more than 45 million pots of yogurt and desserts, the equivalent of 5,680 tons, with 35 employees. The same year, with 51 employees the Huehuetoca plant only produced 3,220 tons. The high tonnage per worker in Belgium, compared with Mexico, is largely the result of the use of one litre pots in Belgium for conditioning, whereas in Mexico only 0.12 litre pots are used. The annual production of the Belgian plant is thus 160 tons per worker as against 63 in Mexico, a ratio of 2.5 to 1.

If we compare employees by occupation, we notice that at the executive level, and for people employed in the preparing and conditioning phases and in operating machines, the numbers are almost equal; 31 in Belgium and 34 in Mexico. The big difference comes from administrative personnel (2 to 7) and laboratory personnel (2 to 5). In addition, in Mexico, two work posts are for mechanics doing small repairs and daily maintenance as well as three work posts for guards. Danone Mexico's personnel and salary breakdown is as follows:

Danone Mexico — Personnel and Salaries

	1974	1975	1976	1977
Total	70	99	126	170
Foreign	4	4	4	2
Salaries (million pesos)	—	5.256	10,173 (14.9% of turnover)	29,920 (16.6% of turnover)

The autonomy of Danone Mexico towards the mother company

The degree of autonomy of the subsidiary towards the mother company is first of all a function of the capital structure of the firm. Let us recall that the participation of the mother company was only 49 per cent, the part of the Mexican partner (after the successive increases in capital to which he could not subscribe) only 11.5 per cent, and the rest, 39.5 per cent, deposited in 'fidéicomis' in a Mexican bank which could not be used in any way in business operations. Consequently, without being in majority control, the mother company has a de facto majority,[3] and could, in practice, control and direct its subsidiary right down to the last detail. This theoretical dependence is underlined by the presence at the head of the firm of the French expatriate, a former executive of one of the firms in the BSN-Gervais Danone group in France.

The recent implantation of the subsidiary in Mexico would also contribute to its greater dependency on the mother company: an important holding in the firm represents, first of all, an investment which has to be profitable and which thus has to be closely monitored, given that a bad start could have irreversible consequences.

The situation would have been completely different if the BSN-Gervais Danone group had been merely content to sell its technology to a Mexican firm, ready to take it back if a minimum annual turnover were not attained.

The autonomy or dependence of the Mexican subsidiary thus seems like an academic question. The problem that this situation raises, a problem which recurs in all discussions and papers concerning the presence of multinationals in developing countries, is really the same for all subsidiaries or multinationals, whether located in developing countries or industrialised countries. We could as easily take the example of firms whose headquarters are in Paris in northern France or Milan or Turin, 'controlling' subsidiaries in the south of France or Sicily. The problem, finally, as it is often debated, is in the ability of any firm whatsoever to establish subsidiaries! From this point of view, it would be perhaps just as well to compare Danone Mexico with a firm in the group located in Marseilles or Belgium.

Nevertheless, the study of the organisation and the management of Danone

Mexico leads to certain conclusions. Despite the absence of a specific study or adequate opinion polls, it appears evident that for the man in the street in Mexico, and even more so in other towns in the country, Danone Mexico seems like a purely Mexican firm. The name of the firm, Danone, if the last 'e' is not pronounced, sounds Spanish. In its advertising, no allusions are made to the foreign character of Danone products which would encourage certain Mexicans to prefer them to Mexican products. (One must not forget the snobbishness prevalent in all of Latin America concerning imported articles, often independent of their actual qualities. In certain circles, the offer of a local whisky or wine could seem like an insult, and any traveller will tell stories of the difficulties he may have encountered in various hotels when he asked to buy local fruit rather than California canned fruit.)

The very low number of foreigners in the firm, only two since the end of 1976, also contributes to reinforce the 'Mexican' image of the firm. Let us say that the environment of the firm, the constant use of Spanish, the salesmen's uniforms, the decor of the delivery vans, the architecture of the new offices of the firm in Naucalpan, the working hours — in fact, all aspects of daily business management are those of a purely Mexican firm.

As against this, regarding aims and strategy, the 'separation of powers' is very evident. The annual budget prepared for Danone Mexico is discussed (the volume of proposed new investments determines the length of discussions), but, as in the case of French firms belonging to the group, the budget can be approved only by the mother company. The same goes for the elaboration of the five-year development plan which is revised and adjusted every year. All the financial exercises having ended up in losses until the end of 1977, it is not yet possible to determine who would finally decide on the distribution of profits or reinvestments, but it is very probable that the opinion of Paris would prevail.

Similarly, the management, control and cost analysis methods which are applied in all the subsidiaries of the group whether in Latin America or in Europe, are those used by the mother company. The model to follow is the end-product of research and improvements developed by the head office over many years. It constitutes a transfer of administrative technology of high value and should be considered as such. To change the argument somewhat; no sensible person would oppose the use of an imported machine which is not available on the local market and which would also be the object of a technology transfer contract approved by the government, under the pretext that its use would be harmful to the purchasing firm's autonomy. However, let us note that in the 'machine' we are talking about now, the model to be followed and even the forms which are used to fill in the monthly report for the mother company are (for reasons of convenience to Paris headquarters) composed in French. For Mexican executives who have only begun to study French, this gives a foreign stamp to the firm.

Once the budget is approved, however, local management is in charge without any interference from the mother company. The autonomy of the subsidiary thus includes fields as varied as they are important: turnover, increases or decreases in production, supplies of raw materials, sale prices of products, advertising, all fixed costs related to the factory or to distribution and transport — in brief, all the elements contributing to gross cash flow in industrial accounting. Similarly, putting new products on the market as well as personnel and social policies, are all responsibilities of local management.

Other functions, including financial charges, are also the responsibility of the subsidiary. In fact, these depend on the relationship between fixed capital and debt (determined by decisions to increase capital or to take out loans) which are decisions taken by the mother company. On the other hand, for operating capital and routine financial management, the subsidiary has its own policies and can take the initiative in dealing with any given local bank. It thus determines by itself its own financial affairs.

Therefore, it is far from coercive remote control on the part of the mother company, and in the very well-defined area of cash flow, the Mexican subsidiary in effect has a much larger autonomy than the group's subsidiaries which are located in industrialised countries. In the final analysis, the autonomy or the dependence of the subsidiary depends largely on the level of competence of the general manager and of his knowledge in communicating with the mother company.

Economic implications of the presence in Mexico of BSN-Gervais Danone

The yogurt market in Mexico — Mexican and foreign competing firms

At the end of the 1960s, the sale of yogurt was not very widespread in Mexico. It was known as 'Bulgarian milk' which housewives sometimes prepared by themselves at home. The first firm to produce yogurt industrially, in 1968, was Derivados de Leche SA, which sold its products under the brand name Delsa. It was a family company, whose capital was 100 per cent Mexican. It did not advertise and its sales network was limited to a few neighbourhoods in Mexico City. The distribution of fresh products such as yogurts requires that sales points be equipped with refrigerating equipment, or at least a refrigerator, which is not the case in all the 'abarrotes' (or little stores) which today still account for the greatest part of Mexico City's food sales.

At the beginning of the 1970s, two factors contributed to the considerable development of the yogurt market. First of all modern supermarkets began to mushroom in Mexico City and other large cities. And then in 1973, a joint venture put on the market a new brand of yogurt, Chambourcy. The firm which produced these yogurts and distributed them, Industrias Alimentacias Club SA, was owned by a Nestlé subsidiary which had been established in Mexico since 1935 (a subsidiary which, with almost 3,000 employees in 1973, was among the largest foreign firms in Mexico's food industry). Know-how and long experience in Mexico, modern production methods, well-established distribution networks, an ambition to take first place in the sector and the means to finance advertising campaigns — all the firm's qualities contributed towards the quick expansion of yogurt consumption.

Nestlé's subsidiary's entrance into this market as the first foreign firm to undertake industrial production of this particular product did not crush Delsa, its only local competitor, in the short term. On the contrary, in the first stage, it reinforced Delsa's position. It is estimated that Chambourcy's advertising multiplied the overall demand for yogurt in Mexico by a factor of 3.5. The Delsa plants, which had been operating at only 50 per cent of capacity, began to work at full capacity as early as the end of 1973. They were even considering doubling their capacity during the following year.

In March 1974, when the first Danone yogurt appeared on store shelves in Mexico City, the market, small as it was, was in full expansion. Here also, statistics show that during the first year, Danone Mexico's sales were not harmful to Delsa; rather, the same thing happened as during the previous year with Chambourcy: that is, a further expansion of the market. Production and sales of all competitors were on the increase.

Various market studies undertaken in 1974 estimated the total demand for that year to be around 2,650 tons. In comparison, sales of yogurt in France during that same year were in the order of 350,000 tons! (Let us note, however, that the French are the world's largest yogurt consumers.) With sales of 163 tons during its first year of production (which was effectively only nine months), Danone took over 6 per cent of the market. During the following years Danone Mexico's progression was constant: 31 per cent of the market in 1975 with sales of 990 tons, and 40 per cent in 1976 with sales of 2,420 tons. In 1977, Danone could not follow the market growth, having insufficient capacity to increase production further. As a result, its share of the market went down to 32.5 per cent even though production reached almost 3,000 tons.

Two new brands were introduced in 1976: Darel and Bonafina, manufactured by Productos de Leche SA, a joint venture with 51 per cent Mexican capital and 49 per cent controlled by Borden, Inc., a US milk producing firm with very active subsidiaries in Latin America. Productos de Leche SA, the largest fresh milk products enterprise in the country, with the most widespread distribution network, had a yogurt production estimated at 900 tons in 1976 and its sales represented about 15 per cent of the market.

We have not yet mentioned a Mexican firm, Zano Alimentos SA, which also sells yogurts under the brand name Cremo, as well as a few other firms not identified in the course of our study which also produced yogurts on a craft-like scale. Their production was very small, 37 tons in 1974 and 60 tons in 1976, or a little more than 1 per cent of the total consumption. Their role in the market is thus negligible.

Table 4.6

The Yogurt Market in Mexico, 1974-77
Production and Shares of Different Competitors
(in tons and percentages)

	1974	in %	1975	in %	1976	in %	1977	in %
Danone	163	6	990	31	2,420	40	2,940	32.5
Chambourcy	1,640	62	1,250	39	1,400	23.5	1,800	20
Darel et Bonafina	—	—	—	—	900	15	2,280	25
Delsa	810	30.5	936	29	1,240	20.5	1,900	21
Cremo and others	37	1.5	34	1	60	1	130	1.5
Total	2,650	100	3,210	100	6,020	100	9,050	100
100% Mexican-owned firms	847	32	970	30	1,300	22	2,030	22
Foreign firms and joint ventures	1,803	68	2,240	70	4,720	78	7,020	78

From Table 4.6, which shows production figures from 1974 to 1977 and the market shares of the above mentioned firms, we can draw some general conclusions. We have already noted that the market penetration of Chambourcy, the first foreign competitor, did not crush Derivados de Leche or Delsa, the only Mexican-owned competing firm. In 1974, the arrival of Danone Mexico, a new firm with foreign holdings, had no decisive effect. The global demand increased because of publicity and because of a certain improvement in the standard of living. Nevertheless, the important fact to notice is the regular decrease in the market share held by the Mexican firm. This share, which was about 30.5 per cent in 1974, dropped to 29 per cent in 1975 and to 20.5 per cent in 1976, then stabilised at about the same level the following year. Taking into consideration that production figures for the same years follow an ascending curve, it is still clear that this increase was less rapid than for the joint ventures. From 810 tons in 1974, the Mexican firm reached only 1,900 tons in 1977, while at the same time Danone Mexico went from 163 tons to 3,000 tons and Darel, in only two years, went from 900 to 2,280 tons.

How can one explain this performance? Pricing policy cannot be blamed: in fact, the sales price of Delsa is slightly lower than the competitors'. However, Danone Mexico's managers feel that presentation and consistency in product quality probably had a definite influence on the consumer. In fact, field studies have corroborated that one of the major preoccupations of the large firms is to succeed in maintaining very high quality standards in order to protect the reputation of their brands.

It is also evident that the lack of advertising by the major Mexican producer also played a determining role. In order to launch new products on the market, Chambourcy in 1973 and then Danone in 1974 did not hesitate to devote an important part of their budget to marketing and advertising in newspapers, on radio and on television. As this campaign concerned a relatively new product in Mexico, Delsa at first indirectly profited from this. Then, as advertising by these new firms became more specific, and the focus shifted from yogurt in general to the specific qualities of Danone or Chambourcy, Delsa, which still did no advertising, quickly lost ground.

It is still difficult to say why Delsa, seeing its situation deteriorate, did not use the same methods as its competitors. Was the firm overawed by modern management methods and more aggressive behaviour on the part of the joint ventures? Did it have limited financial means? Or was it a question of short-sightedness? An analysis of the main stages of development of Danone Mexico has shown that the firm had to resort to two increases in capital since 1973, and that a third influx would probably have to take place in 1977. Moreover, in order to augment its operating capital and improve its industrial plant as well as develop its distribution network, Danone Mexico had to take out important loans in foreign currencies. It is thus possible that Delsa could not or did not want to commit financial resources as important as those of Danone.

But it seems that the key to the analysis lies in the nature of Mexico's small and medium sized enterprises (whose charteristics often resemble those of industrialised countries). The Mexican 'empresario', that is, the owner-manager of a medium sized enterprise of the family type, does not have the same concept of a firm's development as does the expatriate manager of a multinational's subsidiary. The 'empresario' is looking first of all for a quick profit and a personal profit. If he thinks at all about the medium term development of his business, it is often with the idea to sell it, if possible, to a foreign group whose reliability is well-established in the country. This type of Mexican 'empresario' often makes one think of business leaders in industrialised countries towards the end of the 19th or the beginning of the 20th century.

The expatriate manager, on the other hand, applies modern management techniques which he has learned in business school and which he has already practised in one of the group's subsidiaries in an industrialised country. He has the psychological, financial, and intellectual security which allow him to produce losses for several years, if the firm's ultimate objective is long term development. What ever happens he is assured of a place in the mother company. Even if he identifies deeply with his firm, he will never be its owner and the 'marriage', in any case, will be of short duration. Like a monk during the middle ages who specialised in illuminating manuscripts and whom the father superior or the provincial of his order moved from monastery to monastery in order for him to transfer his art to his colleagues, the expatriate manager will stay only a few years at his post. Then another will take his place and apply the same management methods.

Continuity and the financial possibility to work toward the long term development of the firm often constitute a very decisive advantage in a firm's management. In the case under study, a medium sized firm in the food industry, joint ventures seem to be in a much better position than their Mexican competitors. The difference lies not only in the capital's origin (which has no direct bearing on performance), but much more in the management methods with which this capital is linked.

The job market

In order to evaluate the results of BSN-Gervais Danone's establishment in Mexico, one must take into account two factors: the very recent date of this establishment and the modest size of the firm. Danone Mexico, whose industrial production did not begin until March 1974, started with 70 employees. The increase in employees has been constant since then; by the end of 1977 its staff numbered 170 persons. Taking into account the very high rate of unemployment and under-employment in Mexico, the number of these new jobs does not seem significant on a national scale. But in Mexico, every person having a regular income contributes to the livelihood of six other people on the average, and thus effects of this firm's presence cannot be disregarded. Let us also remember that the factory which employed 51 people in 1977 was located in a semi-rural zone where the chances of finding a job are very rare.

Technology transfers

(a) Research and development

BSN-Gervais Danone has three principal sectors of activity: flat glass, packaging materials and food products. For reasons of efficiency and in order to make economies, research centres for each of these three sectors are grouped geographically: the largest research centre for fresh products is in France, in Plessis-Robinson; for flat glass, it is in Belgium. There is no absolute centralisation for the other research units, located in France and in Germany, which support the principal centre.

In Brazil, Venezuela and Mexico, the subsidiaries of course have a 'laboratory' in each plant whose main job is concerned with controlling product quality. In Brazil and in Mexico, where the firms are engaged in food production, this control is very important because the health of the consumers is in question. But none of the subsidiaries in developing countries does research in the proper sense of the word. How could it be otherwise? Research, in order to be efficient, requires human and financial resources which are so large that before anything else duplication must be avoided. In any event, in the case that we are examining, the size of the firm and the priority given to the organisation of production and sales are sufficient reasons to exclude all idea of a research unit on the spot.

Of course, through the technical assistance contract which binds it to the mother company, the Mexican firm disposes of the formulas and techniques developed in research centres or in the group's other plants, provided it pays certain fees.

(b)   Technical and know-how transfer by the Mother Company

Strictly speaking, there is no specific technology involved in the production of yogurts and fresh desserts; it would thus be excessive to talk of technology transfers in the strict sense of the term (from an industrialised towards a less developed country) in this case. There is no doubt that to produce such articles in large quantities, with a constant quality and a high degree of safety, precise know-how and techniques are required as well as experience in the mastering of all modern control methods in order to fulfil these three necessary conditions at an acceptable operating cost.

It is evident that, despite its balance-sheet losses, Danone Mexico has attained these three objectives and thus a transfer of know-how was in fact successfully accomplished. Let us attempt to measure its scope. This type of transfer, especially in the early stages, generally covers all the normal business disciplines: supply of raw materials (notably fresh milk), industrial machinery, and sales and distribution. But Danone Mexico, which buys its fresh milk from a middle-man, does not play a direct role in the gathering of the milk, or in the increase of milk production, or in improvements in cattle breeding or the life-style of the producers. The transfer of know-how is thus focused on production and distribution.

It should be noted that Gervais Danone did not buy a Mexican firm which was already in the business of producing yogurt. The technical services of the mother company thus took in hand not only the construction of a production unit (the most visible part of the project) but also the preliminary studies and the execution of various stages of the project, some of which could be complex. Without listing each one, a few essential steps can be described. First of all, there is the choice of a manufacturing schedule based on a study of the products already existing on the market; then there is an analysis of production and developments in the raw material sector; finally, it is necessary to study the distribution networks which are already operating. Once these facts are known and the partnership with the Mexican partner is formed, a decision must be made on the definition of products, the quantity to be produced and sold, and prices. The different phases of engineering can then be defined: general organisation of the plant, determination of staff requirements, principal guidelines for industrial machinery, blueprints, design of the buildings and peripherals, definition of energy requirements, etc.

The construction phase also demands the permanent presence of several foreign experts as well as several shorter visits by specialists from the mother company to do certain specific jobs such as starting up the production or setting up conditioning equipment and the machinery for cleaning circuits. Parallel to this, the financial management and administration must be organised, staff has to be recruited and technical supervision must be set up. Naturally, technical assistance by the mother company does not stop on the first day of production. It must continue to ensure regular and high-quality production, to maintain or replace equipment or machinery, to make plans for expansion, to launch new products, to maintain efficient management and train personnel, etc.

Without minimising the real contribution of know-how and techniques obtained this way through the channel of technical assistance by the mother company, a few comments are in order. First of all, a general remark: know-how and techniques thus transmitted are goods which are traded against a payment of fees. The additional degree of industrialisation that such an arrangement represents is thus paid, at a certain price, by the host country. Secondly, it is debatable whether the production of yogurt in Mexico, by a foreign firm, is an essential and necessary condition for the country's industrialisation. Yogurt is not a product of prime necessity which cannot be produced by the Mexican milk industry. Technology for industrial production of yogurt existed in Mexico before Gervais Danone's implantation. The 'new' technology brought by the French firm did not create a whole set of upstream or downstream linkages.

Finally, can one say that the know-how and techniques have been definitely acquired by the Mexican subsidary? Only a very, very wise man could answer that question. Let us say that we would have definite proof, for example, if Danone Mexico could set up, without any outside assistance, a new plant in another region of Mexico. The proof would be even more convincing if the real 'Mexican' Danone, with its own resources, established itself in Guatemala or Kenya, for instance. This said, it is clear that the implantation of Gervais Danone in Mexico did cause a technology transfer in the broadest sense of the term, and it is particularly noticeable in the area of professional training.

(c) Professional training

(i) In production. Because of the relative simplicity of the manufacturing process for yogurts — once the installation is set up and operating — technical supervision is limited: in fact, besides its manager, the Huehuetoca plant only requires two high-level technicians: a chief of production who also supervises preparation and conditioning, and the head of maintenance, a mechanical engineer who is helped by two mechanics responsible for day-to-day repairs.

Practical professional training, at the level of technical supervision, was dictated by the need to replace the manager and the chief of production by Mexicans; both of these positions had been occupied by Frenchmen since operations began in March 1974.

The first stage of this training programme in the factory was completed by mid-1976: a Mexican, until then a technical supervisor, was promoted to chief of production, replacing the Frenchman who was in that job and who became the plant's manager. For the new production head, daily practical preparation had been completed in a period of three months, by daily two-hour courses outside the plant. Currently, the new manager involves the production chief more and more in the plant's operation; thus the second phase will be reached in one or two years.

No training takes place in the mother company, local resources being adequate for the required technical level. If need be, the technicians from Gervais Danone can come on the spot and bring complementary know-how.

The region where Huehuetoca is located is essentially agricultural, as we have seen. In the beginning, there was no way to rely on qualified manpower. The training of qualified and unqualified workers had to be done on-the-job, in the factory, except for one mechanic who took daily courses in an outside institution for three months. While the technology that is used is not very sophisticated, some of the machinery and equipment — notably certain conditioning machines — are quite complicated. In addition, quality standards in all respects similar to those of other factories belonging to the group are extremely rigorous since they concern a mass-consumption food product. Under those conditions, the establishment of Danone Mexico in a semi-rural region, despite its relatively low number of employees, constitutes without a doubt, a positive contribution of new techniques.

(ii) In sales. Until 1976, salesmen were recruited according to a strict selection system, and personnel turnover was around 30 per cent. As for previous sales training, it was practically nonexistent. A sales supervisor contented himself with accompanying the new salesman for one or two days on his rounds. By the end of 1976 the firm began to structure itself and hiring of new salesmen began to be undertaken along selection criteria which may seem elementary, but which show how much professional training needs to be developed in Mexico and in this sector.

In December 1976, one advertisement in the newspapaers brought 150 candidates to the Danone Mexico offices. A first selection eliminated 50: those who did not have a driver's licence and those who could not produce a primary school certificate (six years of schooling). The remaining candidates were given a quick test on the four mathematical operations and also took a mental aptitude test. Only ten candidates could be retained.

These new salesmen, before going on their routes, underwent four complete days of sales initiation, the first step in a professional training programme that the firm intends to put into practice during the coming years. At the same time, the two most experienced sales supervisors attended a business management school after hours where they received some basic training twice a week for two hours.

(iii) In administration. In this area, improvement and training first consisted in a long training period to acquaint candidates with the management system

practised in the moth company. Because of the recent establishment of the firm, a complete activity report had to be sent to Paris each month. Simultaneously, the development of a five-year plan, revised and discussed each year, also required a learning period. Even if all that was involved was the adaptation of methods and models of management coming from outside, this training produced positive results in terms of the preparation and competence of local staff. In addition, visits by experts from the mother company, before and after startup, also had a positive learning effect.

Royalties and fees

We have already reviewed elements of the Law of 1972 on Technology Transfers and the Use of Patents and Trademarks (Ley de Transferencia de Technologia y Uso y Explotacion de Patentes y Marcas). This law obliged all firms to register technical assistance contracts between a firm established in Mexico and a foreign entity. The government Commission created to control such activities can give or refuse its permission to register these contracts officially. Restricting as it may seem, this Law has the advantage of establishing clearly, right from the beginning, the obligations foreign investors will have to fulfil.

The Commission has real power over foreign firms as can be shown by the stance it took when the question of fees and royalties to be paid by Danone Mexico to the mother company was taken up. In 1973, the mother company in Paris had signed a contract with its Mexican subsidiary, according to which fees would be 3.7 per cent of net turnover during the first five years, then 1 per cent for each of the following years. The Commission argued that the technology used in yogurt and dessert production was not an advanced technology and did not need to be renewed. It did not accept the proposed rates and instead imposed the following decreasing rates: for 1974, 3.7 per cent; for 1975, 2.8 per cent; for 1976, 1.9 per cent; and then 1 per cent for the following years. In addition, the contract in question had stipulated that the subsidiary should devote 4 per cent of annual earnings to the development and advertising of its brands. The Commission refused purely and simply to agree to this clause.

In 1974, due to losses sustained during this first exercise, the mother company waived its right to royalties and fees.

In 1975, 1976 and 1977, net earnings were 27.5 million, 64.3 million, and 94 million pesos respectively.[4] The amount of royalties, after taxes, was 1,743,000 pesos. In establishing the basis for taxable earnings, royalties are considered as costs and are thus deductible but before transfer they are subject to the tax on profits (Impuesto sobre la Renta) and on sales (Impuesto sobre Ingresos Mercantiles), for a total tax of 46 per cent.[5]

Balance of payments effects

It is relatively easy to determine the influence of Danone Mexico on the balance of payments because it was set up recently and data are still available. In addition, since yogurt is not considered an importable product, the eventual import substitution effect which is always difficult to quantify need not be taken into account.

On the positive side of the ledger are the inflows of hard currency from the mother company, the initial capital input and then the two subsequent increases in capital. From 1973 to 1977, these inflows were over 52 million pesos. Since the firm only produces for the domestic market, the export slot in the ledger remains empty. On the negative side of the ledger one can list, in order of importance: purchases of equipment and raw materials, royalties paid to the mother company and interest paid on foreign loans. Let us note, however, that the mother company waived its rights to royalties in 1974 and also that until now, because of the firm's losses, no dividends have been distributed.

Capital goods which had to be imported because they were not available locally, have been treated as items effectively bought abroad even if these purchases were made through a Mexican import-export firm (whose commissions, however, were excluded from the calculation).

Concerning imported raw materials, the same procedure applies except in the case of powdered milk purchases from Conasupo (a State organisation with a monopoly on purchases of certain foodstuffs from abroad), for which we have estimated that 30 per cent of the powdered milk was of Mexican origin.

Table 4.7

Influence on the Balance of Payments
(in millions of pesos)

	1973	1974	1975	1976	1977	Total
Currency inflows [1]						
Fresh foreign capital (initial subscription and subsequent increases)	+1,000	1,125	15,500	—	35,000	52,625
Currency outflows						
(1) Dividends	— 0	0	0	0	0	0
(2) Royalties for technical assistance	0	0	308	535	900	1,743
(3) Interest on foreign loans	0	0	2,244	2,923	3,711	8.878
(4) Capital goods imports	0	0	800	4,200	11,200	16,200
(5) Raw material imports	0	2,901	2,558	5,444	6,000[2]	16,903
Total Balance	+1,000	—1,776	+9,590	—13,102	+13,189	+8,901

Exchange rates: until end-August 1976: 100 pesos = 8 US $
   since September 1976: 100 pesos = 4.5 US $

[1] Excluding non-capitalised foreign loans (29.4 million pesos at end-1977).

[2] Figures for 1977 not available. Estimate based on 1976 figure, taking into account the increase in production.

61

As Table 4.7 shows, the accumulated balance is positive and shows an inflow of funds to Mexico of about 9 million pesos.

We did not count as inflows of hard currency the loans made abroad to supply operating funds and to finance investments, because these are temporary inputs which have to be paid out again. By the end of 1977, however, these items amounted to more than $1.5 million.

Let us also note that the outflow of hard currency for payments of dividends and royalties was only 1,743,000 pesos for the five years under review, which in terms of return on investment represents around 0.66 per cent per annum. But it should be underlined that the inflows of hard currency were due to increases in capital caused by losses. Once the operation becomes profitable (it seems that this should be the case starting in 1978) there will be no need to proceed to new increases in capital. Going further in this reasoning it is clear that the more the firm prospers, the greater will be its negative effect on the Mexican balance of payments. Of course it is also doubtful that the mother company would continue for long to absorb its losses with new increases in capital.

Notes

[1] This manufacturing process consists of passing a plate of glass over a tin bath. This process allows for obtaining a glass with perfect parallelism and eliminates very complicated mechanical operations.

[2] Table 4.2 does not include in the turnover a sum of 149 million French francs (1.2 per cent of the total turnover) which corresponds to exports to North and South America, Asia and Oceania. The percentages mentioned in the text do not include this figure either.

[3] The annual reports of BSN-Gervais Danone recognise the situation; they indicate in effect that the mother company 'controls' 88.5 per cent of the Mexican firm.

[4] Royalties are paid only on that part of earnings resulting from sales of products with the brand name Danone, and not on earnings from soft drinks and fruit juices sold under the brand name Xalpa.

[5] When the amount to be taxed is inferior to 500,000 pesos, which was the case in 1975, the tax rate is around 38 per cent.

PART III

CASE STUDY: THE 'FIBRAS QUIMICAS SA' CORPORATION

An association between a Mexican corporation, CYDSA SA, and a Dutch Corporation, AKZO, for the production of artificial and synthetic fibres

5   The Mexican Artificial and Synthetic Fibre Industry

Mexican definition of the chemical industry and the petrochemical industry

The expression 'chemical industry' has a particular significance in Mexico, at least as regards the statistical methods that we will have to follow. In this definition, 'chemical industry' does not include primary or basic petrochemistry nor secondary or intermediate petrochemistry, but does include final petrochemistry or the petrochemistry of end products. Given this definition, the branch of the chemical sector which interests us, namely nylon and polyester fibres, for which raw materials are furnished by the petrochemical industry, belongs both to the petrochemical industry and to the chemical industry in the strict sense that we have just described. This is why we are going to consider both of these successively and separately.

The petrochemical industry

Brief description

As can be seen from the following diagram (Fig. 5.1) we can distinguish three steps in the treatment of hydrocarbons. These three steps constitute the three branches of petrochemistry: basic petrochemistry, intermediate petrochemistry and end-product petrochemistry. The petrochemical industry in Mexico is less than twenty years old. The first factories, all with a rather limited production capacity, were built around 1955 but the real boost was given in 1960 by the enactment of a law regulating activities in this sector. This law gave to Petroleos Mexicanos (PEMEX)[1] the monopoly of petroleum products considered as basic raw materials (basic petrochemistry) and left to the private sector, either alone or associated with PEMEX or its subsidiaries, the branches of intermediate petrochemistry. The new law of 1973 on foreign investments repeated the dispositions of the law of 1960: there can be no foreign participation in the primary petrochemical industries, and the foreign share in secondary petrochemical industries cannot go beyond 40 per cent of the capital.

Investments and production

The petrochemical industry is the most dynamic industrial sector in Mexico. Investments in the petrochemical industry went from 250 million pesos in 1960 to 21,000 million pesos in 1974. For PEMAX by itself, investments were 5,020 million pesos between 1971 and 1975 and 3,450 million pesos in 1976, which will

66

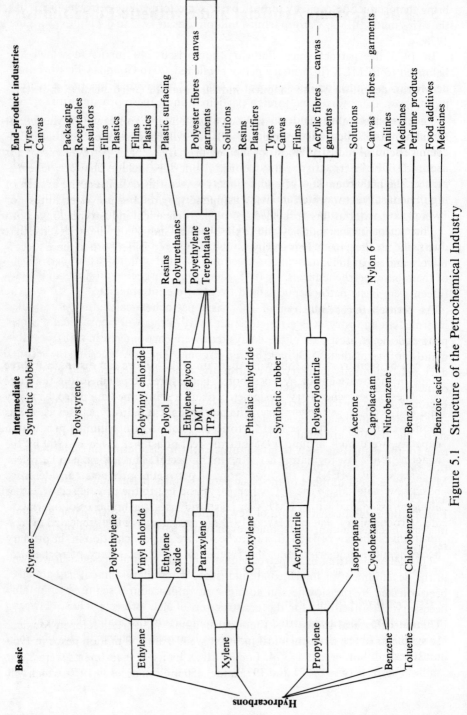

Figure 5.1 Structure of the Petrochemical Industry

bring the production capacity of both basic and intermediate petrochemicals of the firms in the PEMEX group from 4 million tons in 1975 to 6.4 million tons in 1978.

In 1975 the petrochemical industry comprised 246 plants of which 59 belonged to PEMEX (in primary petrochemicals), 20 to Guanos y Fertilizantes de Mexico SA, a nationalised enterprise, and 167 to private firms. In the majority of cases, there was some foreign participation in these private firms.

The figures showing the development of tonnage and value of production are significant. In 1960, production of primary petrochemicals and secondary petrochemicals was 400,000 tons; in 1965 it went to 1,350,000 tons; in 1970 it was around 3,000,000 tons; in 1974, the last year for which we have statistics, it had passed 5,000,000 tons. In other words, the real rate of growth of production during these last years was around 20 per cent per year. The value of production (in 1974 prices) went from 1,040,000 pesos in 1960 to 20,800 million in 1974.

The expansion of the petrochemical industry is reflected in the variety of products and in the progressive vertical integration of basic petrochemicals into intermediates. In 1965, national production consisted of thirteen products, most of them basic petrochemicals. In 1975, there were thirty-five products of which fifteen were basic petrochemicals and twenty were intermediate.

As regards the integration of the basic petrochemical industry into the intermediate industry, it is estimated that by 1978 this will be practically complete and the greatest part of the delays that were encountered in satisfying demand for intermediates will have been overcome. The same goes for the secondary petrochemicals industry as regards the needs of chemical end products, namely synthetic fibres. Moreover, it is probable that around 1980, Mexico will become a net exporter of petrochemical products, principally to Latin America.

It is interesting to ask oneself here why basic petrochemistry got off to a slow start. The reasons are legal, technical and financial. First of all it took a long time for the regulating body to give a sufficiently precise definition of the distinction on which the permissions for participation by foreign capital are based. Moreover, a great number of the basic petrochemical plants built between 1965 and 1970 did not achieve a production volume high enough to be profitable. Finally, the rate of construction of new plants was slowed down by the unusual increase in construction costs, made even worse by PEMEX's lack of financial resources.

This delay in getting basic petrochemistry off the ground caused a slowdown in the development of intermediate industries whose development had already been affected by the slowness in administrative procedures required to obtain necessary authorisations for the construction of new projects. Thus, between 1970 and 1975, Mexico resorted to massive imports of raw materials, and notably synthetic fibres, destined to the different branches of chemical end-product industries.

Technology: foreign dependence

Thanks to the experience acquired in the 1950s in drawing up plans for basic petrochemical plants, Mexican engineering firms today are capable of designing plants for intermediate petrochemicals. Thus PEMEX, with the help of the Mexican Petroleum Institute[2] could draw up the better part of the plans for its own factories, while at the same time having access to foreign technical assistance, if required. Foreign firms are still called in for very complicated projects and also when projects are financed by loans from suppliers of industrial equipment, or when the plants belong to subsidiaries of foreign firms.

The proportion of machinery and capital goods that Mexico can itself furnish for the petrochemical industry varies a great deal depending on production techniques; on the average it is around 15 to 30 per cent. In general, technical assistance from foreigners slows down rapidly once production is underway. It plays a greater role in the end-products industries than in basic and intermediate industries.

An analysis of the petrochemical projects set up between 1970 and 1975 shows a certain tendency to rely upon foreign technical services. In a great number of these projects the construction of the plants was undertaken by national firms. Detailed engineering was executed by Mexican firms in about 50 per cent of the projects, yet basic engineering is still largely performed by the firms that are licensers or by foreign engineering firms.

The chemical industry

(It includes, according to the Mexican definition, petrochemical end-products industries.)

Structure

The chemical industry is ranked second (after the food products industry) in gross value of production, and fourth in number of employees (after the food industry, the textile industry and metallurgy). In 1975, this sector included 1,864 establishments which represented total fixed assets of 25,200 million pesos and a gross value of production of 58,400 million pesos. It employs 122,000 people. (Statistical data which would correspond to these figures for the petrochemical industry are not available.)

Between 1970 and 1975, while the number of establishments actually decreased by about 10 per cent, the number of employed increased by 15.2 per cent, a growth rate superior to that of industry in general (10.5 per cent). The total value of production increased almost 140 per cent in current prices; we estimate that it doubled, at constant prices.

The principal branches of the chemical industry are, in order of decreasing numbers of employees:

pharmaceutical products (37,700 people)
resins and synthetic and artificial fibres (22,050 people), and
cosmetics and detergents (17,500 people).

These three branches represent two-thirds of the production value and employment in the sector. The other branches are fertilisers, basic organic products, paints, oils, fats and diverse chemical products.

Basic *chemical* products (sulphuric acid, nitric acid, phosphoric acid, caustic soda, chlorine, sodium carbonate, hydrofluoric acid) only account for one-tenth of the total production despite an increase, from 1970 to 1975, of nearly 160 per cent.

Foreign participation

In 1970 foreign holdings in the capital of firms in the chemical industry were as follows:

100 per cent of the capital: 56.9 per cent of the establishments;
51 to 100 per cent of the capital: 16.9 per cent of the establishments;
50 per cent or less than 50 per cent of the capital: 26.8 per cent of the enterprises.

In 1970, foreign chemical firms or firms with foreign holdings accounted for 67 per cent of the value of chemical production and employed 40 per cent of the total employees.

In 1970, foreign investments in the chemical industry were estimated at $620,000,000 of which 73 per cent was from the United States. Ten years earlier, in 1960, they had been $362.5 million, of which 81.6 per cent came from the United States. The relative decrease in US investments reflects the entry into the Mexican chemical industry of European firms and notably of German and British firms. We do not yet have the statistics for 1975, however it is clear that foreign investments were on the increase, and that the ratio between national capital and foreign capital has not changed significantly since then.

Let us note that basic petrochemicals which are in the hands of the State represent only about 15 per cent of the total value of petrochemical production, and that the majority of intermediate petrochemical enterprises have some foreign shares in capital.

Between 1967 and 1970, foreign payments for royalties and technical assistance were particularly high and still going up. They went from $24.2 to 37.9 million (+ 50 per cent). They were larger in value than the dividends paid out abroad ($7.3 million in 1967 and $21.5 million in 1970).

A study by the US Congress[3] stated that in 1972 there were 95 subsidiaries of US firms in the chemical industry located in Mexico, and that their financial results were as follows:

Total assets	$763.2 million
Liabilities less net worth	$310.4 "
Net worth	$452.8 "
Sales	$795.2 "
Gross profits	$155.5 "
Taxes on profits	$ 54.7 "
Net profits	$ 62.6 "

On the profit and loss statement, the following expenditures appeared:

Purchases of raw materials	$254.1 million
— of which imported (45 per cent)	$115.0 "
Advertising	$ 39.8 "
Research and development	$ 4.2 "
Royalties and fees for technical assistance	$ 24.1 "

Note the small amount of expenditures in 'Research and development'.

In 1972, exports of these 95 industries totalled $32.9 million. Only the US firms in the Mexican automobile industry did better ($46.5 million). Let us note however, that in terms of balance of payments, the value of exports compensated for only 28.6 per cent of the imports in raw materials.

The artificial and synthetic fibre industry

Among the fibres which are not of natural origin, we can distinguish between artificial fibres based on cellulose, such as rayon and acetate fibres, and synthetic fibres based on petrochemical products such as nylon, polyester and acrylic fibres.

The Mexican artificial and synthetic fibre industry is the most important branch of the chemical industry (not counting, of course, basic and intermediate petrochemicals) in terms of investments (25 per cent of the total). It comes in second place in terms of employment, after the pharmaceutical industry.

This fibres industry started at the end of World War II with the production of artificial fibres. During the last ten years its expansion has been very rapid because of the constant growth in demand for fibres for textiles and industrial usage, and also because of the appearance in the 1960s of the petrochemical industry, which made possible the manufacture of synthetic fibres.

In 1960, the fibres industry had seven establishments and employed 4,200 people for a total production of 500 million pesos. Ten years later the number of establishments had grown to fourteen, employing 9,100 people. By 1975, 17,600 people were working in seventeen establishments with a total production of 7,500 million pesos.

The production ratio between artificial and synthetic fibres evolved rapidly in

70

favour of the latter. In 1960, artificial fibres represented practically 100 per cent of the production; in 1965, 80 per cent; and in 1975, 20 per cent. They will probably account for only 10 per cent in 1981, although between 1970 and 1975, the volume of production of artificial fibres decreased very little (36,000 tons in 1970 and 35,700 tons in 1975). However, during the same period the production of synthetic fibres increased by 240 per cent (from 46,000 tons to 157,000 tons). The increase was particularly marked in polyester fibres for textiles and somewhat less in fibres for industrial use (canvas for automobile tyres in particular).

As could be expected, the entry of artificial and synthetic fibres on the market caused a decrease in the consumption of natural fibres, notably cotton. The annual consumption of cotton dropped from 225,000 tons in 1971 to 175,000 tons in 1974, when the distribution of total consumption of fibres was as follows: artificial and synthetic fibres, 50 per cent; cotton, 49 per cent; and wool, 1 per cent. It is estimated that by 1980, the consumption of cotton will represent only 30 per cent of the total of fibres in use. It is in the textile industry, especially in the modern sector, that the demand for synthetic and artificial fibres and especially for polyester filaments is increasing most rapidly. The craft-like traditional textile industry continues to use cotton.

The considerable growth in investments in the artificial and synthetic fibre industries reflects this evolution: the firm's capital, which was 1,300 million pesos in 1970, reached 2,750 million in 1975 and fixed assets estimated at 3,000 million pesos in 1970, had grown to 8,600 million by 1975. Annual investments, which were around 350 million pesos at the end of the 1960s, passed 1,000 million in 1974 and 1975. All investments during these last ten years were in the area of synthetic fibres.

The production of synthetic and artificial fibres is almost exclusively for the domestic market. Between 1970 and 1975, annual exports were only 75 million pesos on the average, or only two per cent of the total value of production. During the same period, imports averaged around 165 million pesos annually and were greater than exports almost every year; they were particularly high in 1974, 468.5 million pesos.

At the end of 1975, the artificial and synthetic fibre industry comprised nine firms and fourteen plants. The two oldest firms were Celanese Mexicana SA and Cellulosa y Derivados SA, founded in 1944 and 1945 respectively to produce cellulose-based fibres, at least in that first phase. Currently the largest and most diversified firm is Celanese Mexicana. After that, in order of size: Cellulosa y Derivados, Nylon de Mexico, Fibras Sinteticas and Fibras Quimicas, which is the subject of our case study.

Integration of the artificial and synthetic fibre industry into the petrochemical industry

The producers of the most important fibres (nylon, polyester, and acrylic fibres) were almost completely integrated into the intermediate petrochemicals industry between 1970 and 1975. Moreover, because of the expansion programmes which are taking place in basic petrochemicals, the supply of primary products for the synthetic fibre industry should be covered by 1978/79.

As regards nylon, the raw material (caprolactam) is already produced in sufficient quantity by the Mexican firm Univex SA[4] (current capacity: 40,000 tons with expansion projects to produce 90,000 tons by 1978). Also, PEMEX produces sufficient amounts of cyclohexane, the raw material for caprolactam (capacity 85,000 tons).

In the case of polyester, the raw material is DMT (dimethyl terephtalate) produced by Petrocel SA,[5] whose capacity (172,000 tons a year) largely covers national needs. However, the production by PEMEX of paraxylene, the base for DMT, is not sufficient to fulfil national demand. In fact, nobody had foreseen such a rapid progression in the demand for polyester from 1973 to the end of 1975. Moreover, since the Arab embargo on crude oil and the price increases which followed, Mexico had put the accent on petroleum prospecting more than on petrochemical industries. This was a turn-about from the time when Mexico imported crude oil.

Ethylene glycol also counts as a raw material in the production of polyester. It is manufactured in Mexico by two private firms. But PEMAX's production of ethylene oxide base for ethylene glycol, is not sufficient to fulfil national demand. Thus a certain amount still has to be imported.

As regards acrylic fibres, when PEMEX's expansion plans (construction of a plant for the production of acrylonitrile) will be effected, which should be in 1978, production will be completely integrated.

In the case of more recent fibres, polypropylene and polyurethane, integration with the petrochemical sector is not yet realised but this should not take too long in the case of polyurethane due to the construction of the Cydsa-Bayer plant in Vera Cruz for the production of disassociated toluene.

As for the cellulose acetate fibres and viscose rayon, whose production is stagnant, the market is not large enough to justify production of cellulose-alpha which is imported in its entirety. The other raw materials (caustic soda, acetic anhydride, acetic acid, and cellulose acetate) are largely sufficient for the production of artificial fibres.

The National Association for the Chemical Industry (ANIQ) estimates that despite the decrease in demand for polyester which began in 1975 and 1976 because of difficulties in the textile industry, the fibre industry could reach in 1981 a production volume of 330,000 tons, an increase of 60 per cent with respect to 1975. In this case, capacity would have to be increased by 127,000 tons (which concerns only synthetic fibres) and investments would have to be about $400 million. Raw material requirements would then be as follows: acrylonitrile, 70,000 tons; DMT/terephtalic acid (TPA), 183,700 tons; caprolactam, 65,200 tons; ethylene glycol, 66,800 tons; and polypropylene, 12,700 tons.

If the expansion plans of the intermediary petrochemical industry for 1976 to 1978 are effected, that is, if the economic difficulties subsequent to the devaluation of the peso in 1976 do not slow down expected investments, PEMEX's as well as the private sector's, production capacity should at least match national demands.

Notes

[1] The Mexican petroleum industry was nationalised in 1938 and it is PEMEX, a state corporation, which took over from the private firms. PEMEX's monopoly takes in all aspects of the petroleum industry: production, transport and distribution; and since 1960, it also includes the basic petrochemicals industries.
[2] The Mexican Petroleum Institute was created in 1965 to provide technological support to PEMEX. In 1973 the Institute had a budget of 200,000,000 pesos (8 times the initial budget) and employed 1,700 people, of which 60 per cent highly qualified (i.e. university graduates). With the aim (still far away) of building up an independent Mexican technology, the Institute does basic research and applied research. It has training centres, sends students to foreign countries, and invites foreign professors. It also puts its scientific knowledge and technological knowledge at the disposal of other countries in Latin America which produce petroleum and with which it collaborates.
[3] *Multinational Corporations in Brazil and Mexico: Structural Resources of Economy and Non-Economic Power,* Washington DC, 1975.
[4] The Dutch State Mines Corporation (Nederlandse Staatsmijnen) has a 21 per cent share in Univex and furnishes the technical assistance.
[5] The American firm Hercules has a 40 per cent share in Petrocel and plays an important role in the transfer of technology.

6   The Fibras Quimicas SA Corporation

Introduction: AKZO NV, The Dutch mother company

Organisation of the group

AKZO NV, whose headquarters is in Arnhem, Netherlands, is the result of the merger, in 1969, of 'Algemene Kunstzijde Unie' (AKU)[1] and of Koninklijke Zout-Organon (KZO).[2] In its new structure, AKZO is a holding company with about 150 subsidiaries. It holds first place in Europe for the manufacture of synthetic fibres and also has a predominant position in salt extraction.

With a turnover of 11 billion guilders and employing about 91,000 people in 1976, AKZO is one of the largest chemical conglomerates in Europe. Of that total turnover, 35 per cent was produced by firms in the group located in the Netherlands; of the 150 subsidiaries, at least 100 were located outside the Netherlands. It is thus evident that AKZO is a multinational corporation by definition. Table 6.1 shows the main firms in the group according to its 1976 Annual Report. The great geographical diversity of its affiliates shows the high rate of multinationalisation of the group.

AKZO is a holding which holds shares (directly as well as indirectly) in all the firms associated in the group. AKZO is managed by a Board of Managers whose members are jointly responsible for the group's policies.

Its internal organisation is characterised by a breakdown of activities by products within autonomous divisions operating on the international level. Currently, the group has eight divisions, each managed by its own Board with a president at its head. Each division groups together a certain number of firms having the same or related activities, without taking into account their geographical location. Thus, for example, the division AKZO Chemie whose principal products are industrial chemicals, has its headquarters in Amersfoort, Netherlands. The division comprises eighteen firms located in eleven different countries. Chemical fibres are re-grouped in two divisions: Enka Glanzstoff for the European firms (UK and Spain excepted), and AKZO International (with its headquarters in Arnhem) for the firms in the rest of the world, except for the United States.

The liaison between the Board of Managers and the management of each of the divisions is ensured by the presidents of the divisions who are members of the Board of Managers of the holding corporation.

Top management defines the strategy of the group, sets the objectives to be achieved and determines priorities. It delegates power to the managements of the different divisions, which ensures an effective decentralisation of the group.

74

This decentralisation in function is accompanied by a geographical decentralisation: the headquarters of each of the divisions is in a different city. We are thus far from a pyramid-like concentration of power.

We should note in passing that the adoption of this structure preceded the great debates on multinational corporations which hit the scene in 1972/73, both through the media and within a number of international organisations.

The principal products of the AKZO group are: synthetic fibres; salt; basic chemicals; surfacing materials such as paints, lacquers, glues, and coatings; pharmaceutical products; and certain consumption goods such as detergents, household paper and certain food products.

In 1976, consolidated turnover which had reached almost 11 billion guilders could be broken down as follows: synthetic fibres, 35.4 per cent, chemical products 34.6 per cent, pharmaceutical products, consumption goods and other products, 30 per cent.

General activities of AKZO in developing countries

(a)   Reasons for implantation

For AKZO the reasons for wanting to establish itself in developing countries follow from the firm's expansion strategy. Like all conglomerates whose activities spread over several countries, AKZO, in order to maintain its position with respect to the competition, is 'condemned' to spread out more and more geographically and to diversify its production by the creation of new products. Such an expansion is not only the expression of a dynamic company policy, it is before anything else a question of survival.

On various occasions, in documents released to the public, the managers of AKZO have stated these reasons even more precisely: the market in the home country, the Netherlands, is too small to allow for the development of a very large chemical industry (AKZO-Netherlands exports 70 per cent of its production); geographical distribution of investments also reduces risks; the costs necessary for financing research and development are so high that they must be covered by an ever-increasing number of companies which buy the technologies developed by the mother company; and finally, a firm which employed 91,000 people at the end of 1976 cannot go against historical trends: whether we like it or not, the international division of labour is becoming more and more of a fact.

Under these conditions multinationalisation is not strictly aimed at Third World countries, but the geographical limits of expansion which first stopped within Europe and then encompassed the United States, now comprise countries whose economic development — as relative and varied as it may be — guarantees already today a considerable market and represents important reserves for the future.

Table 6.1

Principal companies of the Akzo group

December 31, 1976

*The operating companies are listed by division or Group company
Percentages of participation are only stated for companies in
which Akzo N.V. holds a direct and/or indirect interest of less than
95%.*

Enka Glanzstoff, Arnhem/Wuppertal — Netherlands/W. Germany
*man-made fibres, non-wovens,
plastics, dielysis membranes, film,
machinery and various industrial products*

%	Company	Country
	Enka Glanzstoff B.V., Arnhem	Netherlands
	Akzo Plastics B.V., Zeist	Netherlands
	Enka Glanzstoff AG, Wuppertal	W. Germany
	Barmag Barmer Maschinenfabrik AG, Remscheid-Lennep with establishments in Switzerland, USA and Brazil	W. Germany
49a —	Fabelta N.V., Brussels	Belgium
93 —	Ferenka Ltd, Limerick	Rep. of Ireland
	Italenka S.p.A., Milan	Italy
93 —	Erste Osterr. Glanzstoff-Fabrik AG, Vienna	Austria

Akzo International, Arnhem — Netherlands
chiefly man-made fibres

%	Company	Country
62 —	British Enkalon Ltd, Leicester	U.K.
37b —	Brand-Rex Ltd, Glenrothes	U.K.
58 —	La Seda de Barcelona S.A., Barcelona	Spain
45 —	Cyanenka S.A., Prat de Llobregat	Spain
40 —	Fibras Quimicas S.A., Monterrey	Mexico
40 —	Petroquimica Sudamericana S.A., Buenos Aires	Argentina
40 —	Hilanderias Olmos S.A.,	

%	Company	Country
	Woermann Chemische Baustoffe GmbH, Salzkotten with establishment in Switzerland	W. Germany
67 —	Carbosulf Chemische Werke GmbH, Cologne	W. Germany
67 —	Rhodanid Chemie GmbH, Cologne	W. Germany
	Akzo Chemie, division of Akzo Belgie N.V., Mons	Belgium
	Stikstofderivaten N.V., Mons	Belgium
50 —	Akzo Chemie France S.a.r.l., Compiegne	France
	Akzo Chemie Italia S.p.A., Arese	Italy
	Akzo Chemie U.K. Ltd, London	U.K.
	Interstab Chemicals Inc., New Brunswick, New Jersey	U.S.A.
48 —	Poliquima Industria e Comercio S.A., Sao Paulo	Brazil
50 —	Nippon Ketjen K.K., Tokyo	Japan
50 —	Kayaku Noury K.K., Tokyo	Japan
50 —	Japan Interstab K.K., Tokyo	Japan
50 —	Lion Akzo Co., K.K., Tokyo	Japan
50 —	Akulu Chemicals (Pty.) Ltd, Isithebe	S. Africa

Akzo Coatings, Amstelveen — Netherlands
*paints, stains, synthetic resins,
adhesives and waxes*

%	Company	Country
	Sikkens B.V., Sassenheim	Netherlands
	Kon. Talens B.V., Apeldoorn	Netherlands
	Kunstharsfabr. Synthese B.V., Bergen op Zoom	Netherlands
	Syntac B.V., Voorburg[1]	Netherlands
	Sikkens GmbH, Emmerich[2]	Netherlands
	K.G. Lesonal-Werke Chr. Lechler	W. Germany

No.	Company	Country
49 —	Enka de Colombia S.A., Medellin	Colombia
49 —	Enkador S.A., Quito	Ecuador
44 —	Century Enka Ltd, Calcutta	India
29 —	Nichemtex Industries Ltd, Lagos	Nigeria

Akzo Zout Chemie, Hengelo (O) — Netherlands

salt, chlorine, alkali products, petro-chemicals

No.	Company	Country
	Akzo Zout Chemie Nederland B.V., Hengelo	Netherlands
	Ned. Soda-Industrie B.V., Delfzijl	Netherlands
	Zoutchemie Botlek B.V., Rotterdam	Netherlands
50 —	Methanol Chemie Ned. v.o.f., Delfzijl	Netherlands
35 —	Delamine B.V., Delfzijl	Netherlands
	Norddeutsche Salinen GmbH, Stade	W. Germany
50 —	Elektro-Chemie Ibbenb. GmbH, Ibbenburen	W. Germany
	Konezo, div. of Akzo Belgie N.V., Brussels	Belgium
50 —	Dansk Salt I/S, PR Mariager	Denmark
50 —	Greek Salt Industrial Commercial Ltd, Piraeus	Greece
87 —	Companhia Industrial do Rio Grande do Norte (CIRNE), Macau	Brazil
50 —	Denak K.K., Tokyo	Japan
42 —	Holland Electro Chemical Industries (Pty.) Ltd, Johannesburg	South Africa

Akzo Chemie, Amersfoort — Netherlands

process chemicals and additives for the polymer-manufacturing and polymer-processing industries, organic chemicals, industrial chemicals

No.	Company	Country
	Akzo Chemie Nederland B.V., Amersfoort	Netherlands
60 —	Ketjen Carbon B.V., Rotterdam	Netherlands
50 —	Cyanamid-Ketjen Katalysator B.V., Amsterdam	Netherlands
	Akzo Chemie GmbH, Duren	W. Germany

with establishments in Morocco, Tunisia, Senegal,c Ivory Coast and Cameroun

No.	Company	Country
48 —	Dacral S.A., Paris	France
	Vercolac S.p.A., Milan and Florence	Italy
	Sikkens S.p.A., Dormeletto	Italy
	Colorificio Linvea S.p.A., Naples	Italy
29 —	Ivanow S.A., Barcelona	Spain
	Miluz S.A.I.C.I.F., Buenos Aires	Argentina
49 —	Companhia de Tintas e Vernizes R. Montesano S.A., Sao Paulo	Brazil
55 —	Metropolitan Paint Factory Ltd, Bangkok	Thailand

Akzo Pharma, Oss — Netherlands

ethical drugs

(Organon International B.V., Oss)

non-prescription drugs

(Chefaro International B.V., Rotterdam)

hospital supplies and equipment

(Organon Teknika B.V., Oss)

raw materials for the phamaceutical industry

Diosynth B.V., Oss)

veterinary products

(Intervet International B.V., Boxmeer)

crop protection products

(A Agrunol B.V., Groningen)

Sales offices or production plants of one or more of the above companies are established in:

— the Netherlands, West Germany, Belgium, France, Italy, United Kingdom, Republic of Ireland, Denmark, Norway, Sweden, Finland, Switzerland, Spain, Portugal, Greece, Turkey

— Mexico, Argentina, Brazil,

—	Colombia, Ecuador, Venezuela	
—	Lebanon, Iran, India, Thailand	
—	Indonesia, Philippines, Hong Kong, Japan	
—	Australia, New Zealand	
—	Morocco, Zaire, South Africa	
	Akzo Consumenten Produkten, The Hague	Netherlands
	detergents and cleaning products, paper products, health and body-care products, foodstuffs	
	Kortman & Schulte B.V., Dordrecht	Netherlands
	Otares B.V., Enschede	Netherlands
50	Grada Produkten B.V., Amsterdam	
	Recter B.V., Veenendaal	Netherlands
	Aerofako B.V., Apeldoorn	Netherlands
	Kon. Eau de Colognefabriek J.C. Boldoot B.V., Amsterdam	Netherlands
	Kon. Fabr. T. Duyvis Jz. B.V., Zaanstad	Netherlands
	Kortman, division of Akzo Belgie N.V., Brussels	Belgium
50	Mayolande S.A., Seclin	France
50	Papeteries de Buxeuil S.A., Buxeuil[4]	France
	A/S Blumoller, Odense	Denmark
	Tomten A/S, Sandvika	Norway
51	Lilla Edets Pappersbruks AB, Lilla Edet[4]	Sweden
	with establishments in the Netherlands, West Germany, United Kingdom and Denmark	
65	**Akzona Inc.,** Asheville, North Carolina	U.S.A.
	man-made fibres, salt, specialty chemicals, pharmaceuticals, wire and cable products, leather, foodstuffs and various industrial products	
	American Enka Co., Enka, North Carolina	U.S.A.
	Armak Co., Chicago, Illinois	U.S.A.
	with establishment in Canada	
	Armira Corp., Sheboygan, Wisconsin	U.S.A.
	Brand-Rex Co., Willimantic, Connecticut	U.S.A.
	with establishment in United Kingdom and Canada	
	International Salt Co., Clarks Summit, Pennsylvania	U.S.A.
	with establishments in Canada and the Netherlands Antilles	
	Organon Inc., West Orange, New Jersey	U.S.A.
	with establishments in Canada	

Other companies

50	Silenka B.V., Hoogezand (glass fibres)[5]	Netherlands
19	N.V. Verenigde Istrumenten-fabrieken Enraf-Nonius, Delft (medical equipment, etc.)	Netherlands
	Akzo Engineering B.V., Arnhem	Netherlands
	Feldmühle A.G., Rorschach (adhesive tape)	Switzerland

a participation 49.6%
b affiliate of British Enkalon Ltd (60%) and Brand-Rex Co. (40%). total participation of Akzo N.V., 63%
c participation less than 95%.
[1] will be sold in 1977.
[2] to be included in Deutsche Akzo Coatings GmbH in 1977.
[3] sold to Robert Bosch GmbH at January 1, 1977.
[4] sale to Ncb (Sweden) to become effective in 1977.
[5] participation of Azko N.V., to be reduced to $33^{1}/_{3}\%$ on account of participation by N.V. Noordelijke Ontwikkelingsmaatschappij

(b)   The main lines of the company's policy towards developing countries

For AKZO the basic notion is integration, through joint ventures, with existing local structures. In a second phase, AKZO is not opposed to the idea that this association lead to the establishment of an 'open' company in which a part of the shares, officially listed on the stock market of the host country, would be held by the public.[3]

In a speech delivered at the end of 1973 during a seminar on the 'structures of tomorrow's corporation', the President of AKZO summarised the advantages which his firm could obtain from such an attitude towards developing countries as follows:

1 Local participation not only in capital but also in management allows the firm to adapt itself rapidly to the conditions and possibilities offered by the host country.
2 The local firm, while maintaining links with the mother company, acquires a certain independence and becomes more and more responsible for its performance.
3 The local firm and the mother company must necessarily establish commercial relations between themselves.
4 Such an independence allows the local firm to determine by itself and for the attention of its local Board of Managers, the possibilities for distributing profits.
5 The local firm should publish in its own country its own annual report.

The President of AKZO estimated that such an organisation brings about a greater transparency and constitutes the best weapon against the attacks of the enemies of MNCs: people would thus be able to judge on the evidence the repatriation of profits, the rate of payments for technical assistance, the amount of taxes, and the internal transfer prices between associated firms.

(c)   Magnitude of the group's activities in developing countries

The position of AKZO's management having thus been specified, let us briefly analyse the magnitude of the activities of the group in developing countries. Table 6.2 shows, by regions and for the years 1975 and 1976, quantified data on the group's activities. This table indicates that the share emanating from developing countries is small. The group's sales in these countries (local production + exports from the mother companies in industrialised countries) represented about 7.5 per cent of the total turnover for 1975 and 8.4 per cent for 1976. This percentage is a little higher for certain other items in the same years: for invested capital, 9.7 per cent and 10.7 per cent; for employment, out of a total of 108,000 people, 12 per cent and 13.3 per cent.

Even if the magnitude of these percentages is large because of the volume of

Table 6.2
The Akzo Group in the World
(consolidated and non-consolidated firms)

Breakdown between industrialised and developing countries
(in millions of guilders)

	Turnover				Invested capital				Employees			
	1975	%	1976	%	1975	%	1976	%	1975	%	1976	%
Common Market	7,828		8,596		5,201		4,897		75,600		69,100	
Other — Europe	885		932		660		573		8,500		8,300	
North America	1,949		2,197		1,553		1,433		16,200		15,600	
Sub-total	10,662	92	11,725	91.1	7,414	89.8	6,903	88.8	100,300	87.5	93,000	86.2
Rest of the World[1]	935	8	1,155	8.9	849	10.2	871	11.2	14,400	12.5	15,000	13.8
Total	11,597	100	12,880	100	8,263	100	7,774	100	114,700	100	108,000	100
Industrialised Countries[1] (Total + Japan + South Africa)	—	92.5	—	91.6	—	90.3	—	89.3	—	88	—	86.7
Developing Countries[1] (Rest of the World — Japan — South Africa)	—	7.5	—	8.4	—	9.7	—	10.7	—	12	—	13.3

[1] In 'Rest of the World' are included Japan and South Africa. Since Akzo does not publish separately figures for these two countries, the firm told the author he could figure the contribution of these two countries to be about 0.5% of total turnover.

business which they represent, nevertheless, in absolute value, it is in the industrialised countries that the group undertakes the largest portion of its activities. Thus, in the specific study on the Mexican firm Fibras Quimicas SA, in which the AKZO group holds 40 per cent of the capital, the reader should always keep in mind the very relative importance of AKZO in developing countries.

AKZO and the production of synthetic fibres in developing countries

AKZO's history of establishment of synthetic fibre production in developing countries began in 1959 in Latin America, when the Mexican group CYDSA SA was looking for a technology supplier for the local production of synthetic fibres. A contract between the two firms resulted in the instituting of a new firm, Fibras Quimicas SA, in which CYDSA SA would have 60 per cent of the capital and the Dutch group 40 per cent. The good performance of this joint venture and the financial and technical expertise of AKZO encouraged the Dutch mother company to follow up its interests in this part of the world: in 1964 in Colombia, in 1967 in Argentina, in 1968 in Brazil, and in 1973 in Ecuador. Its establishment in India occurred in 1968 and the most recent to date, in Nigeria, took place in 1975.

We saw earlier that for AKZO, multinationalisation was a necessity. In the realm of synthetic fibres we must underline that for the establishments cited above, in four cases it was a question of AKZO responding positively to a request for technology. In the three other cases the procedure was different; AKZO had large cash assets and was looking for investment possibilities in developing countries; with the major criteria being the perspective of a growth market and the existence of tariff regulations favourable to local industrial production.

Table 6.3 shows, for 1976, statistical data on the total activities of AKZO in the realm of synthetic fibres in developing countries. These data show that turnover increased to 597 million guilders, or 4.6 per cent of the total turnover of the group. Personnel reached 8,600 people, or 7.9 per cent of the total employed by the group, which is 108,000 for all companies consolidated and non-consolidated.

Let us also emphasise that with the exception of a Brazilian firm, Polyenka SA, where AKZO had 51 per cent of the capital, AKZO had a minority share in all the other firms, from 29 per cent in Nigeria to 49 per cent in Colombia and Ecuador.

Let us also note that Table 6.3 concerns only the production of synthetic fibres, depending on the section 'AKZO International'. Other AKZO products were manufactured on the spot or exported from Europe long before 1959. Thus in 1940, Organon, which was going to become, through mergers, one of the largest firms in the AKZO group for pharmaceutical products, had established a first production plant in Brazil. Similarly, in Mexico, beside the production of

Table 6.3
Akzo and the Production of Synthetic Fibres in Developing Countries — 1976

Country	Name of firm	Akzo's share in capital (%)	Date of implantation	Principal products	Turnover (million guilders)	Personnel
Argentina	Societe PSSA	40	1967	DMT	68	1.400
	1. Petroquimica Sudamericana SA			Polyester fibres		
	2. Hilanderias Beccar SA			Continuous polyester textile thread and polyamide polyester thread		
	3. Hilanderias Olmos SA					
Brazil	Polyenka SA	51	1968	Continuous polyester thread	91 production starting in 1978	1.000
	Cobafi SA	45	1974	Industrial continuous polyamide thread		100 (1978: 900)
Colombia	Enka de Colombia SA	49	1964	Polyester fibre	129	1.300
				Continuous polyester and polyamide thread		
				Continuous industrial polyamide thread		
Ecuador	Enkador SA	49	1973	Continuous polyester textile thread	19	300
Mexico	Fibras Quimicas SA	40	1959	Continuous polyester and polyamide textile thread	215	2.700
				Continuous industrial polyamide and polyester thread		
India	Century Enka Ltd	40	1968	Continuous polyamide textile thread	28	500
Nigeria	Nichemtex Industries Ltd	29	1975	Industry for textile filaments, weaving and finishing. Polyester fibres	47	1.300
				Total	597	8.600

synthetic fibres (which is the topic of this case study) other divisions of AKZO also had shares in firms which were making pharmaceutical and veterinary products. The fact remains that of the 8.1 per cent of the group's turnover (consolidated and non-consolidated) coming from developing countries, the sales of locally produced synthetic fibres represents half.

The Mexican group CYDSA SA, AKZO's majority partner (60%) in Fibras Quimicas SA

The firm Fibras Quimicas SA is a part of the Mexican chemical group CYDSA. The group is composed of CYDSA SA, a holding firm with a capital of 290 million pesos and twenty or so subsidiaries. In 1975, CYDSA was twentieth in the list of Mexican firms by sales (2,866 million pesos; Celanese Mexicana SA, the principal competition of CYDSA in the fibre sector, occupied the eighteenth place with a turnover of 3,055 million pesos).

CYDSA's principal products, with their share of the national market, are as follows:

Continuous polyester textile thread (FQ)	:	30%
Continuous polyamide textile thread (FQ)	:	11%
Continuous polyamide industrial thread (FQ)	:	50%
Acrylic fibre (Cellulosa y Derivados)	:	51%
Rayon textile fibre (Cellulosa y Derivados)	:	35%
Industrial rayon fibre (Cellulosa y Derivados)	:	85%
Cellophane (Cellulosa y Derivados)	:	63%
Chlorine and caustic soda (Cellulosa y Derivados) - and Industria Quimica del Istmo — northern zone	:	52%
southern zone	:	33%
Polyvinyl resins (Policid): in suspension	:	23%
in pulp	:	83%

CYDSA holds the majority of shares in all of these firms; as we saw earlier, according to the law of 1973 no foreign firm could hold the majority of shares in a Mexican firm. Moreover, the maximum legal foreign holding was reduced to 40 per cent in the intermediary petrochemicals sector. As far as Fibras Quimicas is concerned, only the operation of polymerisation of polyester belongs in this secondary sector, such as it is defined in Mexican law.

Within the CYDSA group, foreign firms have holdings in a number of subsidiaries (including some of the largest); these holdings have been inevitably brought about by a need for technical assistance. At the end of 1976, the foreign holdings were as follows:

CYDSA subsidiaries	% Foreign holding	Foreign group
1 Fibras Quimicas SA	40	AKZO
2 Celulosa y Derivados SA	10	British Cellophane
3 Policyd SA	40	Goodrich
4 Quimica Organica de Mexico SA	35	Goodrich
5 Quimobasicos SA	49	Allied Chemical
6 Cydsa-Bayer SA	40	Bayer

The association of Celulosa y Derivados with British Cellophane, which is about thirty years old, was historically the first. The latest is Cydsa-Bayer, whose plant for the production of TDI (toluene dissociated for the production of polyurethane) is in construction in Vera Cruz at present. Besides these various joint ventures, CYDSA also negotiated a number of technical assistance contracts with foreign firms, for example the one signed by Celulosa y Derivados with Mitsubishi for the manufacture of acrylic fibres. (This contract replaced an agreement with Rhône-Poulenc which was considered unsatisfactory.)

The Mexican group, therefore, has long experience in joint ventures with several large foreign groups, all competitors in other markets. The relationship between a Mexican majority partner and a foreign MNC minority shareholder is of course very different from the relationship described for Danone Mexico, or other joint ventures, where the local partner cannot carry its weight either technologically or financially with respect to the foreign investor.

Association and technical assistance contract between Fibras Quimicas and the AKZO group

Fibras Quimicas began to produce in 1961. Until then CYDSA, whose origins go back to 1941, had produced only rayon and certain chemical products related to rayon (sulphuric acid (H_2SO_4), sodium hydroxide (NaOH) and carbon disulphide (CS_2)).[4]

When other firms began to manufacture nylon in Mexico, CYDSA decided to do the same and began looking for a partner who could bring in the necessary technology. After having made contact with numerous American and European groups, CYDSA concluded that the best partner would be the Dutch group AKZO NV, which was then known as Algemene Kunstzijde Unie NV (AKU).

Thus a deal was closed between CYDSA and AKU for the production of nylon for textiles and industrial nylon. AKZO (AKU) accepted a share in capital of 40 per cent in the new firm when it could have gone up to 49 per cent. In fact it was AKZO's first experience in Latin America and the Dutch group wanted to limit its risks. (As performance might indicate, AKZO had cause to regret its prudence later on.) The association of AKZO with Fibras Quimicas was followed by several other joint ventures in Latin America (Argentina, Colombia, Brazil, Ecuador). The initial capital for Fibras Quimicas was 45 million pesos. AKZO's 40 per cent share was brought in largely in kind, through manufacturing licences and know-how.

Why did CYDSA prefer a joint venture with a share in capital rather than a simple technical assistance contract without participation, as it did in other cases? Different factors come into play when such a choice is to be made. First of all, the infusion of capital can be a more or less important element depending on the financial situation of the firm, and of course, when he has a financial stake the associate is more involved in the firm. But the essential factor is technology. If we are talking about a technology which can be substantially improved, that is, a technology which is not final, then the choice of partner is important. Finally, the question of machinery and industrial equipment plays a large role. In effect, the engineering services of AKZO designed and built the machinery, which can in turn be adapted to new manufacturing processes discovered or refined by the research centres of the group. Thus, because of its association, Fibras Quimicas automatically got access to the most advanced technological materials.

The technical assistance contract provides that AKZO will supply Fibras Quimicas with the technical services of its engineers and with supervisory services, information, research and development, technological know-how and the necessary set up for the training of personnel. It will also put at the disposal of the firm the required specialists to equip and start up the plant. AKZO in effect commits itself to making Fibras Quimicas take advantage of the best techniques and machinery, given the practical and economic status of the Mexican firm. The price paid by Fibras Quimicas for this technical assistance is a percentage of net sales.

In the whole AKZO group expenditures ascribed to the research and development department, which develops new technologies, represent in general about 3.5 per cent of total turnover. For 1976, this percentage was as high as 3.8 per cent. Fibras Quimicas's level of payments to the Dutch group for technical assistance is of approximately the same order of magnitude.

Production

Fibras Quimicas's production evolved in stages. It started with nylon textile fibres and industrial fibres, first without polymerisation since polymers had to be imported from Europe. In 1968 polyester fibres were introduced. In 1962, Fibras Quimicas employed about 350 persons and in 1976, 2,700. Sales grew steadily: from 20 million pesos in 1962 to 1,300 million in 1976. One must also take into account that inflation has been very high since 1973, and thus affected the

Table 6.4
Fibras Quimicas SA — Production 1971-76
(in tons)

	1971			1972			1973		
	National market	Fibras Quimicas	%	National market	Fibras Quimicas	%	National market	Fibras Quimicas	%
Polyester textile filaments	14,900	8,530	57.2	32,300	12,398	38.4	53,000	13,579	25.6
Nylon for textiles	14,000	3,092	22.1	16,800	2,890	17.2	21,400	3,094	14.5
Industrial nylon	6,283	2,344	37.3	6,900	2,786	40.4	7,857	3,868	49.2

	1974			1975			1976		
	National market	Fibras Quimicas	%	National market	Fibras Quimicas	%	National market	Fibras Quimicas	%
Polyester textile filaments	65,000	15,325	23.6	72,000	20,076	27.9	67,000	20,570	30.7
Nylon for textiles	21,200	2,653	12.5	19,900	2,437	12.2	22,700	2,701	11.9
Industrial nylon	8,194	3,694	45.1	9,771	4,670	47.8	11,744	6,514	55.5

Note: In this Table, we did not take into account production of polymers or industrial polyester fibres.

figures. Table 6.4 shows, for the years 1971 to 1976, the firm's production, in tons, and its share in the national market.

The end-use of the fibres produced by Fibras Quimicas is either textile or industrial. Nylon for textiles is used essentially to manufacture pantyhose and underwear for women. The principal industrial application of nylon fibres is rope, made in the Fibras Quimicas plant, and according to the particular case may be covered with latex; they are also used in the manufacture of tyres (Goodrich, Uniroyal, Firestone and General Tyre are the principal clients of Fibras Quimicas). Industrial nylon can also be used for the manufacture of high strength canvas for trucks, tents, shoes, etc., and one may add nylon fibres for the manufacture of fishing nets, tennis rackets, etc. Finally, industrial nylon is also sold in a granular form destined for the plastics industry.

Textile polyester fibres are sold either rigid or textured. Texturisation is the operation through which rigid fibres acquire a certain structure designed to make the material more supple and elastic. Texturisation was introduced in 1973 in Fibras Quimicas by the AKZO group. Each year a larger quantity of textured fibres are produced by this firm relative to rigid fibres. In 1976, the proportion was 50-50, with rigid fibres losing ground. For economic reasons, the textile manufacturers prefer to avoid doing the texturing themselves (as this involves additional technical operations). If they do it, it is only to utilise their machinery. Textured polyester fibres serve in the manufacture of all types of outer clothing for men, women and children, while rigid fibres (still used in the manufacture of certain types of clothing) are used especially for making materials for curtains or upholstering.

The national market for industrial polyester fibres is still very small and at this time does not justify the acquisition of special machinery. One machine alone has to warrant an annual production of 1,500 tons. For the 135 tons it produced in 1976, Fibras Quimicas used machines part-time which normally are used for the production of nylon fibres. End-uses are about the same as for nylon fibres (canvas for tyres especially, safety belts, roofs for trucks, transmission belts, etc.).

Sales, performance and financial situation

Sales and performance

Table 6.5 shows Fibras Quimicas' sales by products, for the years 1972 to 1976. These figures show that by far the most sizeable production was that of polyester textile fibres: 20,323 tons in 1976 out of total sales of 29,460 tons. Exports were insignificant: 748 tons of industrial nylon. These were mostly exports to Brazil of canvas for tyres.

As for financial performance, it has been very good since the founding of the firm. Sales, expressed in millions of pesos, practically tripled between 1971 and 1976. Even if one takes into account the acute inflation rate, especially since 1973, which contributed to inflating the figures, such an increase in turnover shows the dynamics and the good management of the firm. For reasons of competition and in order to preserve industrial secrets, we cannot give details on profits and on the net profit margin represented by the percentage of net profits with respect to sales.

In Mexico, it is generally estimated that for a firm producing synthetic fibres, the net profit margin should be between eight and ten per cent. Fibras Quimicas, for these last six years, showed an average margin which compared very favourably to these rates, while varying from year to year. These differences are due to internal and external factors: thus, in 1973, the particularly high profits came about because of an increase in sales: 1973 was the boom year for polyester textile, boosted by the success of the 'double knit' (a method of weaving which became a great fad for women's clothing and men's pants). Since 1975, however, the sluggishness of the market, over-production and the great increase in the prices of raw materials have all produced significant decreases in profits.

Financial situation

The initial capital of Fibras Quimicas in 1959 was 45 million pesos. Of the 18 million pesos representing AKZO's 40 per cent, 12.5 million (or $1 million exactly at the time) was contributed in kind or through patents and technological processes; the other 5.5 million was in cash.

At the end of 1976 the firm's share capital was worth 290 million pesos. Since its foundation Fibras Quimicas has never showed a loss and all the increases in capital were obtained through the reinvestment of profits.

As regards capital assets, i.e. capital plus non-distributed profits, at the end of 1976 they amounted to 2,845 million pesos. Note that this sum also includes a total of 1,226 million pesos as a revaluation of assets. Of the total profits accumulated between 1970 and 1976, 55 per cent were reinvested in the firm; but this was not enough to supply working capital or to satisfy investment demand. Thus loans had to be taken out. Because of the tightness of the Mexican capital market, more than half of these loans, either short or long term, were in foreign currencies, almost entirely in dollars. However, their rates of interest were lower than the rates in local currency. (The mortgage rate in Mexico for first-rate credit risks was 12 per cent in 1975 and this was lower than the usual rate practised for commercial loans.) The advantage of this difference in interest rates is not absolute; in fact, all foreign loans have floating interest rates and the risk of change, which seemed very remote in Mexico, became a sharp reality in 1976 when the peso was devalued.

To complete the general picture of the financial situation, let us add that working capital corresponded in 1976 to about 30 per cent of turnover. In conclusion, considering the relations between the firm's capital, long term loans and fixed assets, we can affirm that its financial situation is without a doubt very healthy. The joint venture between the Mexican partner and the Dutch partner was thus fortunate for both firms.

Employment conditions

The CYDSA group has an excellent organisation which is highly structured and Fibras Quimicas is well integrated within this organisation. It is essentially an operational organisation, separated into product divisions, yet each firm maintains its identity within the whole. Besides these divisions there are corporate services which supply all the divisions.

Although Fibras Quimicas's production is entirely dependent on AKZO's technology, from the point of view of administrative structure it is definitely part of the CYDSA family. The firm employs about 2,700 people (the CYDSA group employs about 7,700), of which 700 have the status of 'employees'. Table 6.6 indicates, from 1972 to 1976, the numbers of workers and 'employees' in the firm as well as the amount of salaries and supplementary indemnities, including distributed profits. The reduction of personnel in 1976 corresponds to re-organisation and rationalisation measures taken to reduce the cost of production and overall expenses.

Table 6.5
Fibras Quimicas' sales by Products
1972-76

	1972	1973	1974	1975	1976
NYLON					
Textile	3,281	3,287	2,633	2,409	2,608
Industrial	2,631	3,801	3,673	4,658	5,362
Polymer	167	284	209	298	419
Total	6,079	7,372	6,515	7,365	8,389
POLYESTER					
Textile	11,724	15,395	14,819	18,408	20,174
Industrial	27	25	140	52	149
Total	11,751	15,420	14,959	18,460	20,323
Total national sales	17,930	22,791	21,474	25,825	28,712
Exports	164	—	—	—	748
Total	17,994	22,791	21,474	25,825	29,460

Table 6.6

Personnel and Salaries
(in thousand pesos)

	1972	1973	1974	1975	1976
Workers	1,505	1,863	2,145	2,208	2,060
Employees	468	558	668	742	703
Salaries	47,628	58,182	88,619	147,498	184,403
Indemnities	16,103	22,386	32,742	46,707	59,591
Profit sharing (8% of pre-tax profits)	7,638	8,831	17,533	10,794	16,522

Source: Statistics provided by Fibras Quinicas to the Ministry of Industry and Commerce.

The workers are classed in ten different categories. Each category corresponds to a daily basic salary which goes from 122.60 pesos for the lowest class to 251.25 pesos for the highest class. The normal weekly schedule is eight hours per day and six days per week or forty-eight hours per week. Overtime is paid at double the rate for the first nine hours and triple after the tenth hour.

The plant operates twenty-four hours a day in three shifts. Each worker takes the night shift in turn. Night shift work is taken into consideration in the basic salary, that is, night shifts last only seven hours while day shifts are nine hours for the same daily salary. Workers are paid each week seven times their daily salary, i.e. they receive 365 times their daily salary in a year.

In addition to the base salary the workers also are eligible for several indemnities in accordance with legal norms:

1 an assistance indemnity which covers absences for all other reasons than work accidents;
2 a holiday indemnity: indemnities vary according to years of service; they are at least five times the basic daily salary for the first year and go up to 19 times for 24 years of service and over;
3 Christmas and New Year: 16 times the basic daily salary;
4 Sundays;
5 holidays.

Thus, taking into account these indemnities (and a minimum holiday indemnity), a worker in the inferior category is paid annually 51,300 pesos and a worker in the top category 105,200 pesos.

The most numerous class of workers (about 530 persons) earn about 71,200 pesos according to the same calculation. Thus, the least qualified workers receive about 4,300 pesos per month and the most qualified 8,800 pesos with the 'average' around 6,000 pesos. The basic salaries are comparable with others paid in the economic region of Monterrey, the town where the firm is located.

Table 6.6 also shows that an average of 700 employees received a salary of 77.6 million pesos in 1976, for a monthly average of 11,100 pesos. At the end of that year, the firm had 663 employees split into 98 high-level employees (administration, etc.), 195 'chiefs' doing supervisory and control tasks in the plant, and 370 others (secretaries, etc.). The level of monthly salaries was comparable to those of other firms in the region of Monterrey.

In 1976 the firm declared to the statistical administration that it had paid out 59.6 million pesos for 'social' items, whether compulsorily or voluntarily. Among these charges came, first of all, social security (19 million). Other important categories included indemnities and allowances for seniority (13.9 million) and contributions to the housing fund, INFONAVIT (8 million; 0.5 per cent of the base salaries is obligatory). Finally, other items concerned expenditures for cafeteria, personnel transport, sports uniforms, cultural activities and training courses (numerous courses and seminars, completely free of charge, are organised within CYDSA at all levels of qualification of personnel). All of the workers are signed up with a single union which itself is a member of the Autonomous Federation of Labour Unions of Monterrey. This Federation is outside the official trade union, CTM (Confederacion de Trabajadores de Mexico), controlled by the government. The relations between the trade unions and the firm are good. There has never been a strike within the CYDSA group. In fact there does not as yet exist in Mexico a workers' consciousness equal to that in Europe. In a developing country where under-employment is widespread and poverty omnipresent, it is much more important for the population to have a job than to organise itself to try and obtain improvements in their employment.

The workers are insured against accidents by social security. For the purposes of working out premiums, firms are classified in five categories according to the risks that each branch of the industry implies. Within each category, social security determines a minimum rate, and average rate and a maximum rate which depend on the index of frequency of accidents and the index of seriousness of accidents. Thus each category of firm (Fibras Quimicas belongs to category III) can lower these indices by the safety standards in practice and thus, at the same time, the premiums to be paid (minimum, average or maximum according to the indices). The indices of frequency and seriousness of accidents of this firm are below the limits applied for the lowest rates.

In 1976 there were sixty-four accidents at the firm amounting to 1,270 lost work days. Large posters placed in the interior courtyards show personnel the number of accidents that have occurred in each month in each division of CYDSA, as well as the records of work days without accidents. These good results, by far superior to the Mexican average, can be favourably compared to those obtained in the factories of the AKZO group in Holland. It seems that they are even slightly superior.

Labour productivity

In a general way the productivity in the firm is comparable to that of AKZO. In principle, the machinery is the same. Of course, as for all the firms in the group, whether established in developed or developing countries, studies are under way to determine the critical point when certain machines will have to be modernised.

In the case of texturing, whose introduction is recent (1972), Fibras Quimicas has the most modern machines with the latest improvements. The process of texturing by friction (1976) brought about an increase in productivity of 50 per cent. It so happens that certain operations are less automated than in other firms of the AKZO group. This is true of the polycondensation process and for the drying of polyester for textured fibres (production of polymers in granular form and drying of granulates) as well as for the transport of granulates. The solutions envisaged will be decided upon when the required investments will be economically justified. Among different factors, the ones which are determinant are the cost of the transport of new equipment to be imported and the cost of Mexican labour which is about five times less than the cost of labour in Europe.

However, thanks to the exchange of information on new technological know-how foreseen in the technical assistance contract, successive improvements are being brought to this operation and the current process is among the most productive. The situation is similar where the operation of extending industrial nylon fibres is concerned (productivity at the firm is still below that of other firms of the Dutch group in this area). In Europe for the same operation, machinery allows for the use of coils 60 per cent greater in weight and thus lessens manipulation within the plants. As against this, in the selection of packaging for textured polyester fibres, the firm compares favourably in work hours per ton with the factories in Holland, the United States and the UK. The same goes for coiling of textured polyester fibres.

Finally, it seems that neither the qualifications nor the capability of Mexican labour are to be brought into question. According to figures from a study undertaken within the group, the comparison of work hours per ton of production showed that the productivity of the firm was somewhat below that of other plants in the group, but from 1975 to 1977, productivity improved by 35 per cent.

During the last few years, the utilisation of machines has always been very high: 90 per cent and close to 100 per cent (in 1976) for textile fibres, and about 80 per cent for industrial fibres. The firm has complete freedom to choose its equipment and machinery, and in particular to buy other machines than the Barmag machines from the AKZO group. Recently, the firm invested in machines made by Scragg, of British origin (for texturing of polyester).

The Mexican synthetic fibre market

We cannot say that there is a special national market for synthetic fibres in Mexico. The products manufactured by the firm are identical to those throughout the world and are based on the same technology. The Mexican market does wield a certain influence in one sense: for example, certain products are not manufactured (sewing thread) because there is no national demand. As for textile fibres, the market is much more dependent on the weaving and garment industries than on fibre manufacturers. In general, Mexican consumer demand for clothing follows American and European trends. However, one must take into account certain local customs as well as the climate. The orientation of demand affects the fibre industries in their choice of raw material (polyester or nylon) and in the definition of quality standards required from the fibres. Thus in 1975, the Mexican buyer clearly preferred polyester filaments [5] (23.7 per cent of total fibre consumption, the highest percentage in comparison with other countries).

In a specific case, Fibras Quimicas undertook a marketing study at the consumer level; the company wanted to know the market potential for rugs in which nylon fibres would be used instead of rayon fibres. The preliminary conclusion was negative. This study was done by specialised local professionals in Mexico City working directly for CYDSA's corporate services, which are at the disposal of all the divisions in the group.

Besides this unit in Mexico City, the fibres division of CYDSA also includes a proper marketing department which itself is divided into three departments: textile filaments, industrial filaments, and short fibres. (Fibras Quimicas does not produce short fibres.)

Textile filaments production is not aimed at large volumes but rather at superior quality, specialisation and product variety; this is even more true in the case of nylon filaments, where the market is dominated by the competitor Celanese, than for polyester filaments. Fibras Quimicas holds a very good position (40 per cent of the market) for fabrics called 'Pie y Trama' which require a very high quality thread. With its new factory in Querétaro, Celanese will increase its market share in polyester textile filaments. The price of these fibres being rather variable at this moment, Fibras Quimicas is not interested in defending its position and in increasing its production capacity.

The industrial fibres market (canvas for tyres especially) is more straightforward than for textile fibres. The products are standard and change much less rapidly than do textiles which are subject to trends of fashion. Fibras Quimicas and Celanese share this market approximately equally.

Fibras Quimicas does very little advertising — much less than Celanese — and when it does any at all it rarely mentions the name of CYDSA, rather emphasising the brand names under which the products are sold. Thus the brand name TERLENKA, during the great double-knit boom, was associated in the public mind with all clothing made of polyester in general. The firm has the right to use free of charge AKZO's brand names, of which TERLENKA is one. Under these conditions, the name 'Celanese' is much better known than 'CYDSA'.

The firm's policy does not aim at exports. The best prices are to be found on the Mexican market, and the firm's products might not be competitive on other markets. However, it does happen that if equipment is not being used to full capacity for the national market, the firm does fit in some production for export. But this is not the extent of the firm's effect on the Mexican export market. There are also indirect effects: for instance, the national production of nylon textile fibres has effectively made imports almost unnecessary. On the other hand, there were no imports when the production of polyester textile filaments began in Mexico, which means that national production created a new need. For both nylon and polyester the increase in consumption of synthetic fibres coincided with the decrease in cotton fibre consumption. In turn, this resulted in the sizeable increase in cotton exports during the last few years. In the case of industrial fibres, nylon progressively replaced rayon.

Weaving technology for synthetic fibres is fundamentally the same as for natural fibres and rayon, and was already known in Mexico. In both cases the weaving requires the same types of machines. However, for nylon and polyester fibres there are certain techniques to be learned and applied (temperature controls, humidity control, operating speed of the machines, dyeing of fibres, etc.). At the beginning, technical assistance provided by Fibras Quimicas to its clients was thus very significant. The special department in the firm which was responsible for this is much smaller now; textile industrialists have assimilated the technical assistance that they received and do not have recourse to this service except when a new quality of fibre is introduced on the market.

In Mexico City CYDSA's divisions have the use of a laboratory for analysis to help clients resolve their day-to-day problems. This is not a research department, and no basic research takes place in Mexico. This laboratory has weaving looms for client demonstrations. Occasionally, Fibras Quimicas also receives from AKZO samples of new materials. Before going on the Mexican market they have to be tried out in the laboratory in order to teach the required techniques later on to the fabric manufacturers. This laboratory is also used to handle customer complaints. In any case, the firm does not limit itself to imitating the samples that AKZO might propose; it carries out its proper experiments, tries out new mixtures of fibres, etc.

Fibras Quimicas does not have any distributors; sales are made directly to the textile industries. Most of the salesmen are textile engineers and for several years now all newly recruited salesmen have had to be engineers. Once hired, the salesmen must pass a training phase first in the laboratory in Mexico City and then in the factory. They work in different production divisions but not in different firms (note that the CYDSA fibre division also includes a part of the producers of Cellulosa y Derivados SA).

Technology transfer

We have seen that the establishment of the synthetic fibre industry in Mexico is relatively recent. In 1960, production of artificial fibres (cellulose, rayon, acetate fibres) represented 100 per cent of non-natural fibre production. At that time, the Mexican group CYDSA was already on the market with its rayon production and with chemical products related to rayon. For the managers of CYDSA (who had predicted the rapid decline of rayon in the early 1960s) it became an urgent matter to associate themselves with a European or American partner who had the know-how, the knowledge of manufacturing process techniques and the required technology to produce synthetic fibres on the spot, in order to maintain the group's position in the Mexican market.

This is why the technical assistance contract finally concluded with AKZO reflected the major preoccupation of the Mexican partner: to make sure that the inputs of required technology would be such that the production of synthetic fibres would be rendered possible, and that this new technology would be quickly assimilated. Almost eighteen years have now passed and the Mexican partner has mastered perfectly the techniques and the manufacturing processes concerned.

In the first years of the joint venture, the number of Dutch technicians permanently detached to Mexico was much greater than today. (There was only one left at the end of 1976.) Trips by experts, in both directions, were more frequent. In accordance with the contracts, stages of specialisation in the group's factories in industrialised countries were organised for the Mexican specialists. Thus, in order to prepare the start-up of the firm, a group of twenty-five Fibras Quimicas employees, engineers, technicians, manufacturing supervisors, qualified workers and others, were sent to the Netherlands where they stayed for three to four months according to the individual.

Today the objective is not only to produce synthetic fibres, but to improve the manufacturing processes which exist, to rationalise management and to adapt machinery for possible new products. Thus the channels of transfers of know-how and technology have changed substantially. Now the work is levelled at the analysis of ways to eliminate bottlenecks and control quality, since basic manufacturing processes are well in hand.

The services furnished by the Dutch group can be summarised in the following manner:

1 All the available know-how, knowledge and processes in all the firms in developed countries which belong to the synthetic fibre division of AKZO are at the disposal of the Mexican partner.

2 The results of ongoing research as well as all new processes or industrial machinery developed by the firms in the group are also brought to the attention of Fibras Quimicas.

3 The same goes for other services such as organisation, programming, maintenance of the machiner, marketing, pollution problems, etc.

This service is not limited by the fact that AKZO has only 40 per cent of the capital in the firm: it is available in its entirety just as for other subsidiaries of the group in which AKZO has a majority interest.

This transfer of knowledge takes place during visits by Dutch experts to Mexico or experts from the firm in the group's factories in Europe as well as the United States; in addition, AKZO organises seminars in Arnhem especially for the Mexican firm to help solve particular technical problems; and finally, the Mexican engineers participate in seminars which are convened regularly to discuss problems of productivity, production organisation and sales and marketing techniques.

Over the last ten years a system of reports emanating from the research services of the group has been perfected. These reports, sent to each of the affiliated firms, do not only deal with research and engineering but include as well precise descriptions of all new improvements in all the plants and research centres of the group. Practically speaking the Arnhem centre functions as a data bank; it receives from each of its research centres and affiliated firms a constant flow of information which it re-distributes to all the firms which are tied in by a technical assistance contract.

In the opinion of the Mexican partner, this open-ended system of technical assistance has great advantages. The technical information which flows into the Mexican firm without prior request takes in a much wider area than could be covered by simple answers to precise questions asked by the firm's technicians. Thus the flow of available information which may not be utilised immediately by the Mexican plant nevertheless constitutes a reserve of knowledge which is always on hand and which ultimately amounts to a library that the Mexican technical services can consult regularly.

This method is even more profitable to the Mexican firm given that its technical executives, competent and well-prepared, are not content to merely passively take in the data they receive: these data are discussed, eventually adapted and sometimes improved, as in the case of the polycondensation operation.

The transfer of technology from AKZO to Fibras Quimicas consists fundamentally in applications of basic research carried out in the research centres of the Dutch group. The Mexican firm does no basic research; there is no doubt that given the structures of the firms and the political and economic relations between industrialised and less-developed countries, the Mexican firm is not large enough and its market is too limited to be able to finance the investments that would be required to establish a research department *per se*. It follows that without any basic research the firm could not, by itself invent new products and would even run the risk of no longer maintaining its competitiveness. Nor could it buy on the international market the advanced technology which it would need, since it is known that in most cases, any technology which can be bought is already obsolete.

In the general conclusion of the study, we will look at the consequences of this state of affairs.

Taxes

Fibras Quimicas also contributes to the economic life of Mexico through the taxes it pays to the State. We have seen that the firm has never shown any losses, thus taxes on profits have always been considerable.

Direct taxes

For the years 1972-76, the amount paid in taxes on profits was 325 million pesos (of which about 17 million on accountable profits corresponding to re-evaluations of stocks.)

In addition, AKZO paid a direct tax of 42 per cent on payments received under the technical assistance category, as well as 20 per cent on repatriated dividends.

Note that Dutch legislation considers the sums corresponding to technical assistance as profits. In order to avoid double taxation this amount is deductible from taxes. But, as the Dutch rate of taxes is superior to the Mexican rate by 6 per cent, AKZO has to pay out the sum corresponding to this difference. As for dividends received from abroad, which have already been taxed in their country of origin, they cannot be deducted but on the other hand they are not taxed again.

Indirect taxes

In 1972, the firm paid the State 14.6 million pesos representing sales tax (impuesto sobre ingresos mercantiles). From 1973 on, this tax, which was 4 per cent, was passed on to the clients and the firm paid out for them the sum of 158 million pesos between 1973 and 1976. The same rate of 4 per cent is also applicable to royalties paid by AKZO for technical assistance but is paid by Fibras Quimicas. For export sales, this same tax of 4 per cent of course cannot be passed on to clients, but the amounts paid are minimal (about 2 million pesos from 1974 to 1976). Besides this tax on sales, the firm must pay several other indirect taxes, of which the most important are those on salaries (impuesto sobre nominas, impuesto casa habitacion or INFONAVIT) and which from 1972 to 1976, represented a total of approximately 42 million pesos.

Fibras Quimicas also paid 55.4 million pesos in the 1972-1976 period for social security.

Fibras Quimicas was never exempted from taxes on profits, either totally or partially. However, it did obtain reductions of 75 per cent during five years on that part of the sales tax which was already collected by the State of Nuevo Leon, where the headquarters and the factory are located. (The 4 per cent tax was earlier composed of two taxes, one the 'Estatal' of 1.422 per cent and the other, Federal, of 1.8 per cent.) The firm also benefited, until 1974, from reductions of 65 per cent on the machinery import tax, and of between 40 per cent and 50 per cent on the raw material import tax (caprolactam, DMT and glycol), as long as the national production did not suffice. Now there is no longer any fiscal exemption.

The government has encouraged exports of products of which at least 60 per cent of the cost is of local origin (which is the case for the firm's products), by an incentive of 11 per cent calculated on the sales price at the factory (ex-CIF). This incentive is exempted from the 4 per cent sales tax. Since the devaluation in September 1976, the government has suspended this incentive.

Balance of payments effects

It was impossible to analyse the balance of payments for each year going back to the beginning of production in 1961. We could not find all of the data, especially those that had to do with imports of raw materials (which were much larger then). What we could establish is simplified and shown in Table 6.7, covering the years 1972 to 1976. The Table indicates for this period a negative cumulative balance of 550 million pesos, or US $43 million.

The following remarks are indicated:

1 For that entire period, imports of machinery, equipment and raw materials, represented 61 per cent of the currency outflows. The other 39 per cent were payments for interest on loans taken out abroad, payments of dividends on the capital and payments for technical assistance.
2 These imports of machinery and raw materials could not be avoided, since they were not available locally. We shall see further that from 1974 on, the national Mexican production of DMT, raw material for polyester production, and of caprolactam, raw material for nylon, allowed the reduction in, and then finally the elimination of all imports — which explains, in the Table, the very noticeable decrease of these imports starting in 1975.
3 We did not take into account in the Table inflows of currency concerned with loans made abroad for operating capital and for financing investments, because these were temporary inflows which would flow out upon repayment.
4 Note that in 1961 the initial capital of the firm was 45 million pesos and that of the 18 million representing AKZO's 40 per cent, 12.5 million had been brought in through patents and the other 5.5 million, or US $440,000 in

cash. This sum of $440,000 was an inflow of currency which does not appear in our Table. All the other successive increases in capital having been effected through re-investment of profits, there were no other inflows of hard currency in that sense.

5 Table 6.7 also does not include outflows of hard currency related to the initial purchases of machinery and equipment for the plant in 1961 (machinery and equipment which were still productive in 1972, the year where our Table begins). It was not possible to find out the amount paid in currency for each import of equipment since 1961. However, we can estimate it in the following manner: as the production machinery was not available locally, it had to be imported almost in its entirety; we therefore took the value of machinery and equipment on the balance sheet at the end of December 1976, 926.7 million pesos; we deducted everything that wasn't production equipment (office machines, etc. which were bought locally); of the 738.7 million pesos remaining, we also deducted 30 per cent for installation costs; there remained 517.1 million pesos, or a little more than US $41 million. This amount should thus be taken into account as an outflow of hard currency in order to have an overall idea of the situation.

Table 6.7

Balance of Payments
(in thousands of pesos)

	1972	1973	1974	1975	1976	Total
Imports						
Machinery and raw materials	30,395	66,182	146,723	60,767	55,015	359,082
Other currency outflows						
Technical assistance	19,311	28,947	55,013	59,661	64,934	227,866
Dividends						
Interest						
Other						
Exports	⟨3,100⟩	⟨813⟩	—	⟨66⟩	⟨32,218⟩	⟨36,197⟩
Net Balance (negative)	46,606	94,316	201,736	120,362	87,731	550,751
In thousands of US$	3,728	7,545	16,138	9,628	5,995	43,034

The controversial problem remains of how to estimate the impact of import substitution of synthetic fibres brought about thanks to the local production of the firm. This problem seems too theoretical to attempt a quantitative estimate, which would be the object of so many unverifiable assumptions that it really would not have true meaning. AKZO's management did not share this viewpoint. We do not wish to start a debate, especially since we think that there has not been such a thing as import substitution for many years now; but we shall present AKZO's position, without comment.

They estimate that a measure of import substitution is a reality and that it reduces, cancels or reverses the negative balance of payments on Table 6.7. They also admit that it is difficult to quantify this 'effect'. They point out that the firm's sales from 1972 to 1976 (calculated at average international prices) were five times the negative balance. Admittedly, some items should be deducted, namely local purchases of raw materials; they do not pretend that the resulting amount would be significant, but they estimate that it should be taken into account when calculating the effects on balance of payments of a firm like Fibras Quimicas.

Some remarks

Considering the eighteen-year relationship between CYDSA and AKZO in Fibras Quimicas, we can offer the following conclusions.

First of all, from the viewpoint of objectives it is clear that the joint venture has been a success. The Mexican firm had to find a partner willing to manufacture in Mexico a new product which required, at the time of start-up, an advanced technology. For the Dutch group, the objective was two-fold: first of all to sell technology, and secondly to make a profitable investment. All the goals have been attained: the production of synthetic fibres has become almost a routine, and the financial performance of the firm has always been positive.

In the second place, from the viewpoint of economic results and effects, the firm has shown the traditional effects of a firm which works well and whose twenty years of activity are a credit to the history of progressive industrialisation in Mexico: it has created new jobs, improved the standard of living, increased professional training, substituted for imports and brought about confidence in the competence and seriousness of the local partner.

The development of the synthetic fibre industry has had repercussions on the intermediate petrochemicals industry. It has brought about the production of certain raw materials within the country. Until 1972, caprolactam, raw material for nylon, was entirely imported according to needs. Since then the production of Univex, a Mexican firm with 79 per cent local holdings, progressively substituted itself for imports and finally eliminated them. From 1972 to 1976, Fibras Quimicas' needs in caprolactam, calculated according to the production of nylon, were respectively 5,800, 7,200, 6,900, 7,100 and 9,200 tons. (The annual production capacity of Univex is 40,000 tons.) In turn, the production of caprolactam triggered off the production by PEMEX of cyclohexane, and then of benzene for the production of cyclohexane.

The same goes for DMT, the raw material for polyester, for which Fibras Quimicas' needs from 1973 to 1976 were successively: 13,900, 15,900, 20,700, and 21,000 tons. There was a need to import until 1975, when another Mexican joint venture, Petrocel, began to produce DMT in Mexico. (Fibras Quimicas' demand represents about 11 per cent of the annual capacity of Petrocel.) Moreover, during the same period, the firm required (for the manufacture of polyester) almost 24,000 tons of glycol, now also produced by PEMEX.

Along the same lines, we can also mention purchases of packing cartons from the Mexican firm Tital of Monterrey, purchases which represented, with 35 million pesos in 1976, about 1.3 per cent of the national production of cartons.

But what was most noticeable in this joint venture was the degree of real autonomy which the Mexican partner achieved. In the realm of production, autonomy is certainly limited by the industrial machinery which comes almost entirely from abroad. We must also note that in order to encourage local industrialisation, the law stipulates that only goods which are not available in Mexico, whether they are for production or consumption, can be imported. As against this, all the installation work for equipment and machinery was performed by Mexican firms and Mexican labour, as was the construction of the buildings. For construction of the plant and the set-up of equipment and machinery, only seven technicians came from Holland. After start-up, that is after 1961, there were never more than two or three Dutchmen in the firm and a technical director, who came at the beginning and has remained in Monterrey. The general manager has always been a Mexican.

We saw earlier that for manufacturing itself, techniques and processes had been completely absorbed. As for internal organisation and work methods — financial management, accounting, as well as personnel and social policies of the firm — these are really CYDSA's. It goes without saying that the language used is Spanish.

In fact, the firm is not a subsidiary of AKZO but of CYDSA, who effectively not only holds the majority of shares but imposes its decisions on its minority partner when it feels that its interests so demand. The composition of the Board of Managers reflects this relationship: the ten seats are split between four non-Mexicans representing AKZO and six Mexicans representing CYDSA, among which the president.

Notes

[1] Firm founded in Arnhem, The Netherlands in 1911.

[2] Firm resulting from the merger in 1967 of two corporations of which the principal branch was founded in 1887.

[3] This ultimate phase cannot be envisaged for all developing countries and certainly not for the least developed among them which do not dispose of a sufficient capital market.

[4] For the production of rayon, in addition to the raw material, which is cellulose, one also requires products such as H_2SO_4, NaOH and CS_2. This is why several years after its founding, and with the aim of integrating, CYDSA decided to produce for sale these chemical products as well as the chlorine obtained in transforming sodium chloride into sodium hydroxide.

[5] The term 'filament' is used to distinguish it from short fibres.

7 Conclusions

The circumstances which led AKZO to buy into a Mexican firm were very different from the ones described for BSN-Gervais Danone. In the latter case it was a question of the French firm wanting to establish a subsidiary in Mexico and looking for a Mexican partner for a joint venture starting from scratch. In the former, we are talking about a large Mexican firm, CYDSA SA, already highly structured, calling on a foreign MNC to furnish the technology which it needed to diversify its production.

Also, the manufactured products are not comparable. Danone Mexico put yogurts and prepared desserts on the market whose manufacture did not require sophisticated technology. In fact, it was simply a question of handling and know-how, so as to ensure a regular quality in the product: in the food industry, quality control is essential, because finally it is the health of the consumers which is in question. But the fact still remains that before the arrival of Gervais-Danone in Mexico, there already existed a Mexican firm without a foreign partner which was manufacturing yogurts and prepared desserts whose quality appeared to satisfy the Mexican consumer.

As against this, for reasons of technology (in 1959 as well as in 1976) a Mexican firm wishing to produce synthetic fibres could not do so without technological help from a foreign firm. It is true that thanks to the exchange of manufacturing processes and to the absorption of the required techniques by Mexican experts over nearly twenty years, Mexico today could very well produce, by itself, polyester fibres of a very high quality. However, and we will return to this later, it seems that the Mexican industries in this branch did not develop a basic technology capable of ensuring the manufacture of new products. We know that in this area, technological changes are rapid and no Mexican firm could actually risk cutting the links with the sources of basic research, which is being carried out in laboratories in the United States, Europe and Japan. Whether they want to or not, Mexican firms will have to associate themselves for quite some time with the large MNCs such as AKZO, Dupont de Nemours, British Cellophane, Mitsubishi or Rhône-Poulenc. In any event, licensing agreements are constantly being entered into by the large MNCs in industrialised countries.

But these are not the only differences. Danone Mexico is a food industry firm which manufactures a final product. The multiplier effects of the activities of the firm are thus more constrained than in the case of Fibras Quimicas, a transformation industry of intermediate goods whose activities require, downstream, the co-operation of textile firms for the garment industry and of firms making tyres. As for multiplier effects upstream, we have seen that Danone Mexico does not play a significant role in the production of its own basic raw material, fresh milk. In fact, as opposed to certain firms in the milk products sector which play an active role in the creation and development of milk districts all over Mexico in order to ensure a supply of regular fresh milk, Danone Mexico, because of its small size, buys the fresh milk which it needs from an intermediary. At best, one could say that Danone Mexico, because of the quality of milk required from the supplier, forces him to constantly improve the quality of his supply from milk producers. Let us note that even in this case, milk being a living matter, the visible results of an improvement in the quality are never spectacular. All the specialists in matters of milk production are unanimous on this point: in order to change a herd, improve the race of the stock, arrive at a more balanced feeding system for the animals, accustom the peasant to take care of his cows in an adequate way, milk and then conserve the milk in good conditions until its delivery to the factory — an attitude is needed which implies many changes, and this may take years to show even a minimal result.

For Fibras Quimicas the multiplier effects upstream are more easily definable. We have seen that the needs in raw materials of the firm, caprolactam and DMT among others, helped national firms or joint ventures in the secondary petrochemicals sector to produce, by themselves, raw materials which had been imported until then. In turn, the production of caprolactam led PEMEX to manufacture benzene and then cyclohexane. If a 'snowball' effect was thus produced, it goes without saying that it was not only because of Fibras Quimicas' presence on the market: other Mexican competitors participated actively in the development of the national petrochemical industry.

Neither are the sizes of the two firms comparable. Danone Mexico began its production only in 1974. Two years later it had 200 workers and employees. On the other hand, since its first year of production Fibras Quimicas already had 700 employees, which then grew to 2,700 by 1976. Furthermore, Danone Mexico's turnover in 1976 was 66 million pesos while Fibras Quimicas had already reached 1,200 million pesos.

Let us add that in the two cases the import substitution effects made possible by the local production of both firms is also very different. In fact yogurt and prepared desserts do not constitute a basic need, and Mexico would not have had to import them, even more so given the fact that they were already being produced in Mexico. For synthetic fibres, however, the situation must be viewed from an entirely different angle, since no other Mexican firm could have produced them without a technological input from abroad. Of course, we could argue indefinitely the question of whether Mexico would have had a vital need to import polyester fibres if they were not produced locally.

For all these reasons, we cannot here compare the respective advantages of these two firms or measure the influence that they have had comparatively on the economic development of Mexico.

It seems thus more interesting, in the light of the two case studies presented, to make some comments not on the investments of MNCs in Mexico, but rather on the relation between Mexican development policy and the presence of these firms in the country.

Mexican development policy and the activities of the two firms studied

The notion of a development policy or of a development model is relatively recent in Mexico. Let us say right away that until the 1970s, there existed only an industrialisation policy, although it is true that for a long time, at least at the government level, there was no distinction between industrialisation and economic development.

In the nineteenth and the beginning of the twentieth centuries, there existed some elements of tariff policy to protect the activities of national transformation industries. It is only after World War II that there began to emerge the more specific lines of an industrialisation policy, based before anything else on the promotion of industries favouring import substitution. The Mexican Government at that time wanted to reduce the country's dependence towards the outside, to promote the creation of new industries which would contribute to the generalised growth of the industrial sector and finally, to improve the balance of payments.

This forced industrialisation policy, which seemed at that time like a panacea for all the socio-economic problems that were to be solved, did not have any particular rule relative to the costs of such an industrialisation. Thus, neither the competitiveness of the national industries with respect to the world market, nor the promotion of a national technology, constituted an objective in planning national industrialisation. Nobody was aware at that time, that to put up tariff barriers or purely and simply to forbid imports of raw materials, would not incite the national firms to improve the quality of their raw materials or to lower their costs of production. The result was that joint ventures between national firms and foreign firms were highly desirable. With this background, in 1959 CYDSA began looking abroad for a partner who could bring it the technology it lacked to begin manufacturing a new product. The activities of the new firm would contribute to the sought-for industrialisation, even more so since the firm intended to hire a considerable number of workers. It is clear that AKZO's 40 per cent holding in Fibras Quimicas followed perfectly the official policy of development which had been decided upon by the government.

The establishment of Gervais-Danone in Mexico, at the beginning of 1973, could also fit into the framework of this industrialisation policy, although because of the nature of the manufactured products — neither exportable nor susceptible to substitute for imports — it was before anything else the creation of new jobs accompanied by a certain amount of professional training which were the determining factors making it a suitable venture.

We should also note here that both cases involved the creation of new firms and not simply the buying out by MNCs of national firms which already existed.

Second phase: the promotion of a national technology

Towards the end of the 1960s, it became noticeable that industrialisation at any cost and the policy of import substitution were obsolete. In fact the margin of possible import substitutions was being reduced and, moreover, the high rate of growth of the urban population seeking jobs risked causing internal political difficulties. Moreover, alerted by university circles and certain manufacturers' associations, the government began to take a close look at the deteriorating balance of payments situation. The size of outflows of hard currency paid out to foreign firms for royalties and fees for technical assistance led the economists close to the government to study even more closely the technical assistance contracts which linked the foreign firms to their Mexican industrial partners.

The results of these enquiries brought the government to promulgate the Law of 1972 on the Transfer of Technology and the Use of Patents and Trademarks. We examined in detail this law's clauses in the first part of this study and will not repeat them here. But let us make some comments on this subject with respect to the two firms that we studied:

(a) Danone Mexico. We already mentioned that the contributions in new technology by Danone Mexico were somewhat limited, mostly because of the nature of the products manufactured by the firm. Its positive effects on the Mexican economy were of another type, and in fact concerned employment creation, industrial decentralisation and professional training.

If the firm indeed achieved high quality-control standards, considerable improvements in the manufacturing processes, and administrative and sales systems that were more efficient, one could still not maintain that Gervais-Danone's establishment in Mexico resulted in the production of articles which local conditions had not allowed beforehand. As for the new products that the firm will put on the market, it is perhaps too early to tell (the firm just recently hit its cruising speed and we cannot say where it will go from here). The fact still remains that the firm conformed strictly to the regulations provided by law; it could not have done otherwise.

(b) Fibras Quimicas. The contribution of real technology seems obvious, for the simple reason that without an association with AKZO (or another MNC in that branch) it is difficult to imagine how synthetic fibres would have been produced in Mexico in 1960.

However, we must make the following remarks. While the *contribution* of technology is real, the *transfer* of technology is not so easily definable. Since 1959, an absorption, by the Mexican partner, of basic technology and of manufacturing processes has taken place: the managers of AKZO as well as of the local firm recognised that by 1976, the Mexican firm had acquired the capacity to manufacture synthetic fibres without the specific help of AKZO. But because of the competition and the need to invent new products and improve manufacturing processes, it is also clear that Fibras Quimicas could not do without a foreign partner.

Without going into further detail let us mention that there is always a certain danger in isolating one argument in a debate without taking into account the entire picture. In fact, the relative failure of the government's import substitution policy brought to light the need to increase competition among national firms. It seems obvious that if Fibras Quimicas decided to split with its partner, the technology absorbed by its engineers would be quickly obsolete and with respect to the world market, the industry would not maintain the desired level of competitiveness.

It thus seems that under current conditions and in the market economy of Mexico, AKZO's presence contributes to the development of the country. What can we do at this stage of development in order to make this simple *absorption* of technology capable of generating its own up to date technology in the future?

The law of 1972 defined, among other objectives, the need to make the Mexican industrialists understand the importance of rapid absorption of technology in order to develop the country. In addition, by requiring the buyers of technology to register all their transfer contracts, thus giving a government body the opportunity to refuse approval for these contracts, the government without a doubt triggered off a beneficial psychological shock.

Until 1972, government policy in matters of technology had been limited to imposing different tax rates on the purchase of technology, according to whether it had to do with royalties for the use of commercial trademarks or payments for technical assistance; but nothing was provided to control the cost in hard currency of these purchases, to examine the specific content of contracts tying Mexican firms to foreign suppliers, or to verify if these technologies were appropriate for the economic development of the country.

It seems that the desired awareness was actually brought about, on the level of the Mexican industrialist as well as on the level, which is just as important, of the MNCs for whom the period of *laissez-faire* is definitely over today.

It is interesting to note that certain Mexican industrialists, who resisted the new specifications of the law when it was promulgated, now react very positively to these changes. They have become aware, over time, that this law gives them a powerful card during negotiations with MNCs and that their bargaining power has increased. In parallel to the promulgation of this law, the Mexican Government created an institution whose objective is to create within Mexico the conditions which would allow the future development of local technology. We are talking about the foundation (also in 1972) of the National Council for Science and Technology (CONACYT) which elaborated a national development plan for science and technology for the period from 1976 to 1982. The plan declared that the development of scientific research and independence in technological matters are of national importance and should be given priority. It postulated that the demand for technology would progressively have to be channelled towards local suppliers and a capacity to absorb, and a capability to create, local technology would have to be created. In order to get to that stage, the plan proposed a series of measures: to adapt and improve imported technology, to refuse importation of all inappropriate technology, to encourage the development of technologies which create jobs and respect the environment and to favour technological growth in industrial sectors and in geographical zones neglected until now. For transformation industries, the plan foresaw a development model which, while assuring a greater efficiency of the production apparatus, would give to small and medium sized enterprises access to technological development. The measures taken into account included the varying levels of development of each of these sub-sectors of industry.

Thus for the non-durable consumer goods industries, a sector still somewhat closed to technology, we will be content to define the medium term needs for technology and to adapt imported technology but only by making very simple changes. For the intermediary goods industries, the objectives would be to increase autonomy in technological matters by progressively substituting imports of technology by local technologies and services. For the durable goods industries and for the means of production (capital goods), the goal would be, in the first stage, to attain sufficient technological capacity to be able to adapt all imported technologies to local conditions, and then to arrive at generating a local technology. The different measures of the plan, whose execution has been slightly delayed because of changes in government which took place at the end of 1976, constitute an excellent criterion by which to evaluate the activities in Mexico of MNCs as well as national firms.

Third phase: regulation of foreign investments

A big step on the path towards national independence in economic matters involved stricter regulation on foreign investments. We will not review in detail the law of 1973 which put these regulations into effect; but in the light of the two case studies let us offer some comments.

The objectives of this law were, eventually, to give to the Mexican partner in a joint venture the control of the firm.

For Danone Mexico, we traced the different stages of development of the firm during which the Mexican partner, who had 51 per cent of the capital in the beginning, ended up with 11.5 per cent in 1976. The French partner still has 49 per cent, as per the law of 1973, while the rest of the shares, 39.5 per cent, are deposited in a Mexican bank in the public sector. From a strictly legal point of view, the effective majority should reside in the shares in the bank, since under the laws in force, the bank in which the shares are deposited has the right to vote these shares. But in reality, according to information received at the bank itself, the bank does not interfere with management in such cases, or even with the Board of Managers, and practically speaking it is the foreign partner who controls the firm. But that is not the question with which we are concerned.

What one must see, besides all judicial or legal consideration, are the power relationships which are established between the Mexican and the foreign partners. At the founding of Danone Mexico, the Mexican partner did not have any experience in the manufacture of yogurts or desserts, nor had he developed a distribution system for fresh products. It was thus impossible for him to impose a management or a business administration which was his own. Therefore it was evident from the start, that almost everything would be managed along a model imported from the outside. It is true that in the first stage, the general manager of the firm was Mexican but, as difficulties mounted and bad results were obtained, he was replaced by a new director, competent and dynamic, trained in one of the firms of the French group.

Fibras Quimicas' case is completely different. The Mexican partner, CYDSA, is a highly structured group, already owning a number of active firms in the secondary petrochemicals sector. Moreover, CYDSA headquarters and plant are in Monterrey, a town situated in the north of Mexico some 250 Km from the US border.

After Mexico City, Monterrey is the most important area of industrial development in the country and the city is reputed for the quality and the competence of its businessmen and managers. Moreover, Monterrey is the headquarters of several financial and industrial groups, CYDSA being one of them, comparable to those in the United States and firmly committed to compete with MNC subsidiaries established in Mexico, on the national market as well as on the export market. In addition, their increasing capacity in local technology constitutes one of the factors of their dynamism and their economic strength.

Let us also note that AKZO's participation is only 40 per cent while the Dutch firm could legally have gone to 49 per cent.

It was evident during this study, in Monterrey as well as at the European headquarters, that the power relationship between the firms was very different. First of all, the technology contributed by the European partner was absorbed over the last ten years. The advice of European engineers, as well as the technical information regularly sent by AKZO, are not received passively. This is real cooperation, but the power as well as the control of the firm are on the Mexican side.

If it is true that, especially in the first phase, the contribution of methods used by AKZO in management, financial, sales and administrative matters was considerable, nevertheless the Mexican firm has today acquired a truly Mexican structure. We are therefore far from the traditional image of a multinational corporation dictating from a distance, by telephone or telex, the paths to be followed by its far-off overseas subsidiary. It should be noted again that at the end of 1976 Fibras Quimicas, which employed almost 2,700 people, only had one executive sent by the mother company. He was an engineer, a high level technician, but one who did not have any decisive influence on the overall administration of the firm.

These various considerations bring us to think that the legislative apparatus set up by Mexico in 1972 and completed in 1973 can only attain its objectives if the development of the industrial structures of the country and the receptive competence of its executives, engineers, managers, and administrators reach a considerable level of development.

Is the Mexican system of regulation of foreign investments and promotion of a national technology an exportable model for other developing countries?

It is very difficult to answer this question particularly because of the great differences in levels of development or under-development in Third World countries. The case of Mexico makes us think that in order for there to be no interference in economic interests defined by the State and those fixed by the private sector on the one hand, and the objectives of the MNCs on the other hand, three essential conditions must be fulfilled. First of all the country must produce a coherent economic development policy; secondly, the government must have set up a series of industrial and technology policy instruments which clearly define the field of action of the foreign firms in order to allow for a peaceful coexistence between private national firms and MNCs; finally, there must exist in the country industrialists and businessmen who will be entrepreneurs. If this is the case — and in many developing countries we are far from this situation — a better balance in negotiating power can be established between the often weak local firms and the large MNCs, as well as between the latter and the government of the host country. At a time when economic nationalism in the Third World is particularly acute, these negotiations should not only be based on the share of foreign investments in new firms but also on the following points which seem to us just as important:

1 The real cost of technology imported by the firms, whether they be foreign, public or private.
2 The conditions and restrictions sometimes imposed on the buyer by the seller of technology.
3 The possibility to buy advanced technology without the buyer necessarily having to accept the exclusive control of the foreign investor.
4 The appropriateness of imported technologies concerning the prioities and economic objects of the developing country.
5 The obligation for private, public or foreign firms to train a national staff

and to sub-contract to local firms services and production of certain goods, in order to create a local technological and industrial capability.

We have many reasons to believe that future relations between MNCs and developing countries will depend on the solutions to the above mentioned problems. The Mexican experience presented during this book as a frame of reference to the study carried out on Danone Mexico and Fibras Quimicas can only confirm this.

Sources and Summary Bibliography

In addition to their Annual Reports and published documents, the two European mother companies put at our disposal many internal documents and unpublished reports. We also examined the financial and technical assistance contracts binding the mother companies and the Mexican subsidiaries. Many interviews were held in the Netherlands and France with executives in both firms. Visit to European factories were organised for us.

In Mexico, during our first trip, we spent three weeks at Danone Mexico's headquarters in Mexico City and three weeks in Monterrey, with Fibras Quimicas. These visits had been preceded by an in-depth, twenty-page questionnaire. A final visit took place at the end of the study for final checks.

For the more general part of the study concerning the overall socio-economic situation in Mexico, we refer to the summary bibliography which only contains the most recent studies and publications.

Bibliography

Araud, Ch., Boon, G.K., Garcia Rocha, A., Rincon, S., Strassman, W.P., Urquidi, V.L., '*La construccion de vivienda y el empleo en Mexico*', El Colegio de Mexico, 1975

Banco Nacional de Comercio Exterior SA, '*Mexico 1976, Hechos/Cifras/Tendencias*', Mexico 1976

Barkin, David, King, Timothy, '*Desarrollo economico regional*', Siglo Veintiuno Editores SA, second edition, 1975

Bassols Batalla, Angel, '*El noroeste de Mexico*', Instituto de Investigaciones Economicas, Universidad Nacional Autonoma de Mexico, Mexico, first edition 1972

Consejo Nacional de Ciencia y Tecnologia, 'Politica nacional de ciencia y tecnologia: estrategia, lineamientos y metas', Plan nacional de ciencia y tecnologia, Mexico, 1976

Fajnzylber, Fernando, Martinez Tarrago, Trinidad, '*Las empresas transnacionales, expansion a nivel mundail y proyeccion en la industria mexicana*', Fondo de Cultura Economica, first edition 1976, Mexico

Green, Rosario, '*El endeudamento publico externo de Mexico 1940-1973*' El Colegio de Mexico, first edition 1976, Mexico

Hansen, Roger D., '*La politica del desarrollo mexicano*' Siglo Veintiuno Editores SA, 7th edition, 1976

Padilla Aragon, Enrique, '*Mexico: desarrollo con probreza*', Siglo Veintuno Editores SA, 7th edition 1976

112

Puente leyva, Jesus, '*Distribucion del ingreso en un area urbana: el caso de Monterrey*', Siglo Veintiuno Editores SA, 3rd edition 1976

Restrepo, Ivan, Eckstein, Salomon, '*La agricultura colectiva en Mexico, la experiencia de La Laguna*', Siglo Veintiuno Editores SA, first edition 1975

Solis, Leopoldo, '*La realidad economica mexicana: retrovision y perspectivas*', Siglo Veintiuno Editores SA, 6th edition 1976

Solis, Leopolod, (ed.), '*La economia mexicana, I. analisis por sectores y distribucion*', Fondo de Cultura Economica, Mexico, first edition 1973

Solis, Leopoldo, (ed.), '*La economia mexicana, II. politica y desarrollo*', Fondo de Cultura Economica, Mexico, first edition 1973

Trejo Reyes, Saul, '*Industrializacion y empleo en Mexico*', Fondo de Cultura Economica, Mexico, first edition 1973

Unikel, Luis, '*El desarrollo urbano de Mexico*', El Colegio de Mexico, first edition 1976

Various aurhtors, '*El perfil de Mexico en 1980*', Siglo Veintiuno Editores SA, vol 1, 7th edition 1976; vol. 2, 5th edition 1976; vol 3, 7th edition 1976

Villa M., Rosa Olivia, '*Nacional Financiera: Banco de fomento del desarrollo economico de Mexico*', Nacional Financiera SA, Mexico 1976

Vilarreal, Rene, '*El desequilibrio externo en la industrializacion de Mexico (1929-1975)*', Fondo de Cultura Economica, Mexico, first edition 1976

Wionczek, Miguel S., Buneo, Gerardo M., Navarrete, Jorge Eduardo, '*La transferencia internacional de tecnologia — el caso de Mexico*', Fondo de Cultura Economica, Mexico, first edition 1974

Wionczek, Minguel S., '*La sociedad mexicana: presente y futuro*', Fondo de Cultura Economica, Mexico, 2nd edition 1974